LIVING YOUR CHRISTIAN VALUES

RALPH W. NEIGHBOUR, JR.

PRACTICAL LEARNING EXERCISES BY CAROL BUMBALOUGH

LEADER GUIDE BY JAMES E. TAULMAN

LifeWay Press
Nashville, Tennessee

© Copyright 1999 • LifeWay Press
Original version published 1984
Revised 1999

ISBN 0-7673-9337-6
Dewey Decimal Classification Number: 248.4
Subject Heading: CHRISTIAN LIFE

This book is the text for course CG-0165 in the subject area Personal Life in the Christian Growth Study Plan.

Unless stated otherwise, the Scripture quotations in this book are from the NEW AMERICAN STANDARD BIBLE. © Copyright The Lockman Foundation, 1960, 1962, 1963, 1968, 1971, 1972, 1973, 1975, 1977, 1995. Used by permission. The Scripture quotation marked NEB is from *The New English Bible.* Copyright © The Delegates of the Oxford University Press and the Syndics of the Cambridge University Press, 1961, 1970. Reprinted by permission. Scripture quotation marked GNB are from the *Good News Bible, the Bible in Today's English Version.* Old Testament: Copyright © American Bible Society 1976; New Testament: Copyright © American Bible Society 1966, 1971, 1976. Used by permission. Scripture quotations marked KJV are from the *King James Version of the Bible.*

For more copies of *Living Your Christian Values,* contact Customer Service Center, MSN 113; 127 Ninth Avenue, North; Nashville, TN 37234-0113; call 1-800-458-2772 (8:00 a.m.-5:00 p.m. CT, M-F); fax (615) 251-5933; or email, customerservice@lifeway.com

For more information on discipleship and family resources, training, and events check website www.lifeway.com/discipleplus

Printed in the United States of America

LifeWay Press
127 Ninth Avenue, North
Nashville, Tennessee 37234-0151

Introduction

LIVING YOUR CHRISTIAN VALUES

How to Use This Book

1. Read the introductory material that follows to get an overview of what you will be learning in this study.
2. Remove the Scripture-memory cards from the center of the book, cut them out, and memorize the designated verses each week. Scripture-memory cards are provided for both the *King James Version* and the *New American Standard Bible.*
3. Set apart a definite time and place to meet daily with your Lord. Sit down with your Bible, a pencil, and this book and use the material to guide those times. Complete only one day's work at a time. Be consistent in your daily quiet time, doing five days of study in this book each week. Read the Scriptures and take time to complete all of the learning activities. They were designed to help you understand and apply to your life what you are studying.
4. Consider participating in a group study of this material. If a group study is offered, the group facilitator can use the leader guide beginning on page 113.

Where Do You Go from Here?

If you completed *Survival Kit: Five Keys to Effective Spiritual Growth,* you learned five basic truths. Each truth helped you become established in your new Christian life. And each truth will help you mature for years to come. These truths are summarized on the fingers of the hand in figure 1.

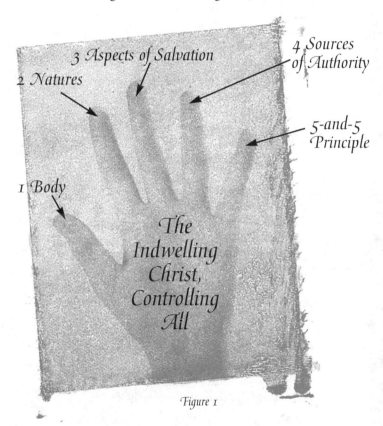

3 Aspects of Salvation

4 Sources of Authority

2 Natures

5-and-5 Principle

1 Body

The Indwelling Christ, Controlling All

Figure 1

Whether or not you completed *Survival Kit*, a review of its major concepts should be helpful preparation for this study. The first official act of the Holy Spirit was to make you a part of the called-out ones. When you became a Christian, the Holy Spirit baptized you into *one body*, the body of Christ. He gave you spiritual gifts, making it possible for you to serve in a special way in that body. Serving in the body is the primary activity of your new life.

In addition, you have two *natures* within you, the old and the new (Rom. 7:25). There are *three aspects of salvation*. First of all, at the time of your conversion you were forever set free from the penalty of sin. Then, because you are the temple of the Holy Spirit, you are continually set free from the power of sin. Finally, when our Lord calls you home to be with Him, you will be set free from the presence of sin.

Further, only one of the *four sources of authority*—the Bible—can be fully trusted. That is because only the Bible is "God-breathed," while tradition, emotions, and intellect are primarily shaped by people, not by God.

You have good news to share! The *five-and-five principle* involves sharing your life in Christ with five friends and praying for five others who are not yet willing to discuss spiritual truths with you.

What Comes Next?

The most important truth of all–You are a minister! Perhaps you have used the word *minister* as a title for pastors. But 1 Corinthians 12 tells us that we are all ministers, and we share equally in the work of ministry.

Ephesians 4:11-12 further explains that pastors are set apart by the Holy Spirit for a very special assignment. They are commissioned to equip each Christian for the work of ministry. Do not think of pastors as the only ones who are ministers. The truth is, all Christians are called to be ministers. You are a minister!

Your ministry includes much more than serving on church committees, teaching a Sunday School class, or singing in the choir. Your true ministry involves serving the persons you are involved with daily. Jesus said: " 'You know that the rulers of the Gentiles lord it over them, and their great men exercise authority over them. It is not so among you, but whoever wishes to become great among you shall be your servant, and whoever wishes to be first among you shall be your slave; just as the Son of Man did not come to be served, but to serve, and to give His life a ransom for many' " (Matt. 20:25-28).

On the Other Hand …

Since becoming a Christian, you have felt a strong inner desire to be a minister. Consider this to be perfectly normal, for Christ's Spirit within you has caused this. Philippians 2:13 tells you that God is working in you, inspiring both the will and the deed, for His own chosen purpose. Therefore, your purpose for living has changed. Before you became a Christian, you chose your own personal goals. Now the deeds you wish to perform come from new desires.

As old values lose their meaning, new values will continually replace them. This book has been written to help you deliberately reshape your personal value system to become that of a true minister. As you grow in Christ, you will throw away old values as though you were discarding worn-out clothing. The old values, in turn, will be replaced by new values—the values of a priest! Look at the illustration on this page. Compare it with the hand on the earlier page. If you studied *Survival Kit: Five Keys to Effective Spiritual Growth,* you learned five basic truths needed to become established in the Christian life. In this book you'll learn five basic values required to become established in your ministry.

As in *Survival Kit: Five Keys to Effective Spiritual Growth,* a picture of a hand will help you remember the five new values of the Christian life. Look at the drawing in figure 2 as you read the following paragraphs. Notice that each new value belongs on a finger of the hand. The first value goes on the thumb.

First of all, you'll learn there is only *one source of significance* for a minister. The saddest thing about not being a Christian is feeling that you have no significance. While you were still a child, you began trying to do something to make yourself feel significant. Years of habits have been formed, all focused on this powerful desire to become significant.

Now as a believer, you have been born as a significant person! No accomplishment can further increase your status or worth, for you are a child of God. What could possibly make you more significant than that? You have become a member of the royal family. You have a guaranteed inheritance. Therefore, you need to rethink and reframe your values about what makes you significant.

Second, you'll learn there are *two views of wealth.* Persons who are not Christians try to become significant by what they

accomplish, because they value wealth as a status symbol or as a source of personal security. Now that you have become a Christian, wealth is no longer a status symbol. It no longer provides any significant security. Therefore, you need to learn a new way to measure the value of wealth: the way a minister values it.

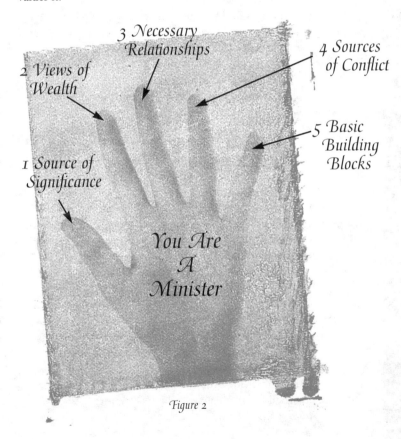

3 Necessary Relationships

4 Sources of Conflict

2 Views of Wealth

5 Basic Building Blocks

1 Source of Significance

You Are A Minister

Figure 2

Third, you will consider how to revalue the *three necessary relationships* in the life of a minister. Before you were a Christian, your relationship with the Father was poorly developed. You may have tried to pray to Him, but it was only to persuade Him to use His power to help you get what you wanted. Now as a minister, you will find how valuable it is to let His power use you so that what He wants can be done through your life. Then your relationship with Christ's body, the church, must take on new value. Before your adoption into it, you were a self-centered person. Now, however, you feel like a person with limbs missing if your relationships with fellow Christians are severed. Finally, your relationships with persons who are not Christians are radically changed. Before you became a Christian, you obeyed the prompting of your own urges, living in sensuality and rebellion against God. Now you are God's child. Being a member of God's family may cause you to become their friend, as Jesus was a friend of sinners.

Fourth, you'll learn about *four sources of conflict:* (1) conflict inside yourself, (2) conflict with others, (3) conflict because of convictions, and (4) conflict between authority and responsibility. If your values as a minister are not clear, the way to handle conflicts may be unclear. As a result, you will be unable to perform your servant work effectively.

Finally, you'll look at the *five basic building blocks* for constructing all future values as a minister. The first three building blocks relate to what is inside you; the last two relate to what is outside you:
1. Your mind: is it master or servant?
2. Your body: is it a temple of the Holy Spirit?
3. Your spirit: is it God-controlled?

4. Possessions: are they yours or God's?
5. People: are they God's or yours?

By letting God's Spirit "guide you into all the truth" (John 16:13), you will find old values uprooted and new ones shaped to replace them. Are you ready? Shall we begin?

The Book with the Answers
The Scriptures are profitable for many things: "for teaching the truth and refuting error, or for reformation of manners and discipline in right living, so that the man who belongs to God may be efficient and equipped for good work of every kind" (2 Tim. 3:16-17, NEB).

In this book Scripture will be used to deal not only with beliefs but also with values. There is a great difference between beliefs and values. Beliefs describe what you know, but your values determine who you are. Jesus referred to persons who used Scriptures to develop beliefs, not values. Jesus said, " 'You search the Scriptures, because you think that in them you have eternal life; and it is these that bear witness of Me; and you are unwilling to come to Me, that you may have life' " (John 5:39-40).

Jesus was talking to Jewish religious leaders, who had diligently studied the Scriptures to develop their beliefs but not their values. Jesus warned that there is a great danger for those who make Bible study an end in itself. Being a Bible scholar on the level of beliefs alone is extremely dangerous. When the testimony of Scripture points to the reshaping of values, personal priorities and preferences must be changed.

In this study you will learn what it means to look at your personal values and to let Scripture guide you to reshape them. Learning activities incorporated in the material will help you do this. Before becoming a Christian, your values were shaped without any thought for the purpose God had for your life. It's important now to let Scripture reshape those values.

The written Word of God leads us to become controlled by our calling rather than simply by our circumstances. Expect to be challenged. Also be aware that the excuses you may think of for holding on to old values are not the true reasons for clinging to them. The reasons probably result from pride, selfishness, and a desire to continue to make all decisions without yielding to God's plan for your life.

The primary Scripture translation used in this study is the *New American Standard Bible*. Scripture-memory cards are provided for both the *King James Version of the Bible* and the *New American Standard Bible*. Feel free to find and memorize Scriptures in another translation if you wish.

Servanthood!

"There arose also a dispute among them as to which one of them was regarded to be greatest. And He said to them, 'The kings of the Gentiles lord it over them; and those who have authority over them are called "Benefactors." But not so with you, but let him who is the greatest among you become as the youngest, and the leader as the servant. For who is greater, the one who reclines at the table, or the one who serves? Is it not the one who reclines at the table? But I am among you as the one who serves' " (Luke 22:24-27).

Perhaps no other Scripture shows more clearly how desperately we need our values changed. The scene was the last supper. All twelve of Jesus' disciples were arguing about who would become the greatest among them. They all expected Jesus to set up His kingdom and give each of them the power and authority to rule over others. This was their attitude at the very time Jesus was saying good-bye to them, only hours from His death on the cross.

Jesus' reply revealed the disciples' wrong values. They all wanted to be great. Why? Because they thought no other way could show that they had personal value and significance. They had not yet learned to prize, most of all, obedience to the Father. Does this Scripture mean that God's servants cannot become presidents or kings? No! They can, because the Father places His servants everywhere. But such a person would serve God while being president. If this truth is unclear to you, this book will help you understand more clearly. For now recognize that Christians were described as those " 'who have upset the world' " (Acts 17:6). Servanthood is one of the values that caused Christians to have that kind of impact on society—and it can continue to have that effect today!

Are you saying to yourself: *If that is what awaits me, I will surely have to rethink my values! Where will I start?* The answer is simple: Start by being honest with yourself. Launch your journey with a willingness to be guided by the truth of Scripture and the power of the Holy Spirit. Hold in question your past values. Examine them to determine whether they have a legitimate role in your Christian life. Be prepared for "old things [have] passed away ... new things have come" (2 Cor. 5:17).

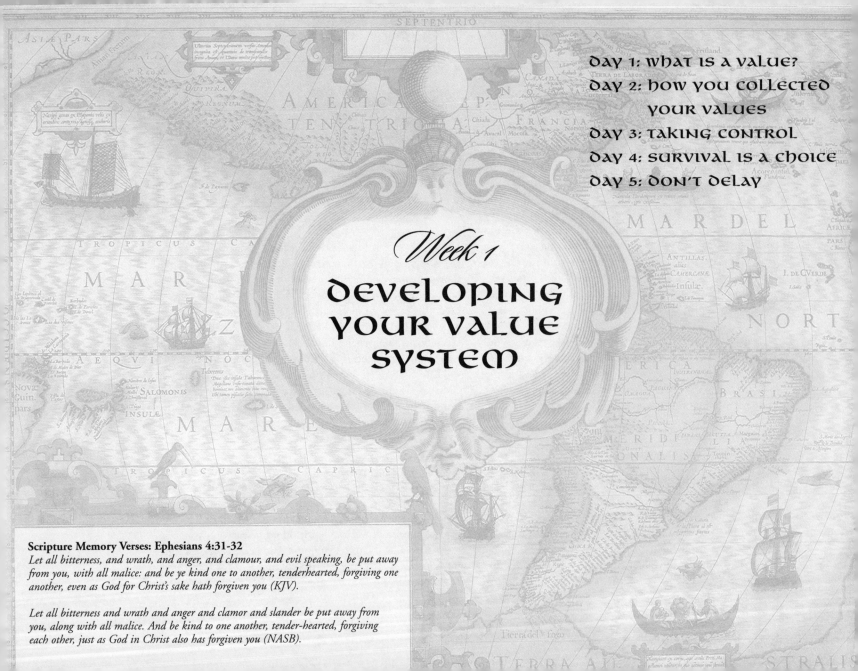

Week 1

DEVELOPING YOUR VALUE SYSTEM

Scripture Memory Verses: Ephesians 4:31-32

Let all bitterness, and wrath, and anger, and clamour, and evil speaking, be put away from you, with all malice: and be ye kind one to another, tenderhearted, forgiving one another, even as God for Christ's sake hath forgiven you (KJV).

Let all bitterness and wrath and anger and clamor and slander be put away from you, along with all malice. And be kind to one another, tender-hearted, forgiving each other, just as God in Christ also has forgiven you (NASB).

WhaT IS a VaLUe?

Use your Scripture-memory card to begin memorizing Ephesians 4:31-32.

Read Ephesians 2:1-7.

A value is something that has great worth to you. When you were born, a "treasure chest" was placed deep inside your life. As a child, you looked around and began to select what seemed to have value. You stored each item in your treasure chest.

You began selecting your values long before you became a child of God. Many of them had nothing to do with your faith in Christ as your Lord and Savior. They were simply collected as you lived, as Ephesians 2:3 says, "indulging the desires of the flesh and of the mind."

From your family members, especially parents, you deliberately selected parts of their lifestyles you considered valuable. Each one went into your inner treasure chest. From friends you selected more values to be treasured. Each time you added a value to your life, you put it in your treasure chest. From your culture, from your textbooks, from media and movies you chose hundreds of values you considered to have worth. Then a strange thing happened. As you grew into a teenager,

your small chest containing treasured values began to grow. You added still more things that seemed to have worth. By now you had forgotten about some of the earlier values you had chosen, but they were lodged safely within your treasure chest. Later in life you discovered that they were still there. It is strange how old values shape new decisions! Into your treasure chest went values related to power, health, sex, wealth, freedom, loyalty, honesty, and so on. You also chose people you considered valuable and discarded others who did not seem to be significant. Emotions that seemed to have value in certain circumstances were selected. Certain habits that seemed to bring pleasure were chosen.

Then one day another strange thing happened. You realized that you could no longer find the treasure chest inside your life! Where had it gone? You looked in all directions. Finally, you found it. Its lid was above you, its bottom was underneath you, and its sides were around you. For a fleeting moment you felt panic. You wondered how long you had been a prisoner inside your treasure chest. The moment of panic did not last long. It was quickly replaced with a warm, fuzzy feeling. You felt insulated, protected, snug within your treasure chest. It gave you a "box" in which to function, with familiar guidelines for behavior. You went on living, using and enjoying all of the items you had chosen to treasure, continuing to reject others that had previously been examined and discarded.

Your treasured values had become you, and you had become what you valued. Unless something unexpected were to happen, you would live as a willing prisoner of your values for the rest of your life!

A value is something that has great worth to you.

"But God ..."! That powerful statement in Ephesians 2:4 explains what happened to you, doesn't it? God touched your life. Suddenly, all of the values you had treasured seemed to be worthless. The value of becoming God's adopted child became one priceless pearl for your treasure chest! What about those old values you stored up before adoption? Do you still live and behave on the basis of them? Have you examined them since the new treasures were placed in your chest by your new Father? Is it time to do so?

Think of your life as a treasure chest with three compartments. In one compartment you placed the values you acquired from your parents. In another you hid the values your friends suggested to you. And in the third you placed values acquired from other sources in society.

My Treasure Chest of Values

Family   Friends   Society

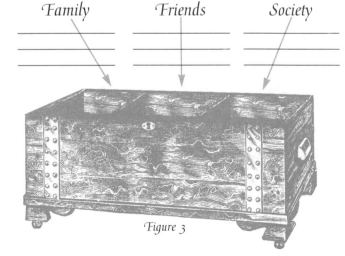

Figure 3

Take a moment now to reflect on your system of values. What specific values did you acquire from your parents and family? List three in the space labeled *Family* in the drawing of the treasure chest in figure 3.

What values did you collect from friends? Especially consider those that are different from the ones your family held dear. Write three in the space labeled *Friends*.

Now think about values you obtained from other cultural sources, such as teachers, coaches, television, books, movies, and popular songs. What values did you acquire from these sources? List three in the space labeled *Society*.

Reread Ephesians 2:1-7. Verses 1-3 describe the way you were before you became a Christian. What kinds of things might have been found in your treasure chest then, according to these verses? List some of them.

_____

_____

You may have listed questionable values and behavior, such as *sin, disobedience, lust, self-indulgence,* and *wrath.*

Now study verses 4-7. What happened to change you and your values?

_____

_____

That's right! God's grace, mercy, and love made you alive in Christ! And not only that, but He also wants to shower the riches of His grace on you! Talk about a treasure chest!

This study will help you look at all of the old values you have stored in your treasure chest. You will examine them, and you will compare them to the new treasures that are being placed in your treasure chest by your Heavenly Father. You will want to cast aside your old values in disgust. You wouldn't dream of putting them back in your chest with the new treasures God is putting there.

Do any of the values you acquired in the years before you became a Christian seem somehow inappropriate now? Carefully look again at the lists you compiled inside your treasure chest. Circle the values that seem questionable.

Day 2

how you collected your values

Francis Schaeffer has said that we thoughtlessly collect our values like germs from life's streets. What does he mean by his comment?

Read Ephesians 4:17-32.

Ephesians 4:17-19 describes the inner character of the non-Christian walking along life's streets, collecting values at random. The mind is concentrating on trivialities. The powers of logic are blinded. There is no contact with God. The inner life is filled with ignorance, lust, calloused emotions, a readiness to test every kind of immorality, and greed. It is as if you were walking down a city street, the wind blowing dust and bits of sand into your face. You breathe some of the dust into your lungs. Your shoes are muddied by a wet, unpaved construction area. You pick up a coin dropped on the sidewalk, rub away most of the dirt and germs on it, and put it in your pocket. You see a tattered old magazine someone has thrown away. Although its subject matter is evil, you pick it up. According to Schaeffer, values are collected in such random ways.

What kinds of values are treasured by such a person in such a situation? Carefully examine Ephesians 4:17-19. List from those verses words that suggest or reflect the values of a person who is apart from God.

_____

_____

_____

You may have listed words like *ignorance, callousness, sensuality, impurity,* and *greed.* Few of these values bring meaning and integrity to life. That is why it is important to sort through the values you collected and treasured before you came to Christ.

God's grace, mercy, and love made you alive in Christ!

Paul instructs us: "In reference to your former manner of life, … lay aside the old self, which is being corrupted in accordance with the lusts of deceit, and … be renewed in the spirit of your mind" (Eph. 4:22-23).

Have you obeyed this verse? If not, the old values collected before you became a Christian and the new values collected since you became God's child are all being stored together in your treasure chest. The ones collected like germs off the street are like time bombs. They will explode when you least expect it and cause great harm to you or to others.

Have you already observed Christians displaying mixed values? If you have not, you will! You will unexpectedly observe a mature Christian practicing a habit that has been carefully hidden from view. For example, you may be driving past a theater showing X-rated movies and see a "mature" Christian buying a ticket. Lust, secretly treasured for years, has caused this "mature" person to slip inside the theater. You ask, How could that person do such a thing?

Still another individual living with contradictory values may confuse you by switching from Christian generosity to selfish greed in a business deal. You will feel that you have been used by this Christian, and it will hurt! You will be surprised by this unexpected change in conduct when money became the issue, and you will become wary of this person's motives.

While at an office party you may be surprised by the conduct of a fellow church member. You may unexpectedly drop in to visit a Christian friend and be surprised by the trashy paperbacks in the den. You ask, How can this be?

The answer lies deep within these persons' treasured values. They have never deliberately examined old values, collected like germs off the street. Furthermore, if you do not examine your old values, you will become like them! There must be a deliberate, intentional process of sorting through randomly selected values. Get rid of the ones that are like time bombs. Leave room for no surprises.

Look at the deliberate, intentional way this is to be done, according to Ephesians 4:22-32: "Lay aside the old self … be renewed in the spirit of your mind … put on the new self … [lay] aside falsehood … do not give the devil an opportunity … steal no longer … let no unwholesome word proceed from your mouth … do not grieve the Holy Spirit of God … let all bitterness and wrath and anger and clamor and slander be put away from you, along with all malice." Old values do not just disappear. They are to be deliberately discarded. Germs off the street have no place in your treasure chest!

In verses 22 and 24 Paul mentioned a key concept, one you're familiar with as a Christian, the concept of the old self and the new self. Look at the two drawings in figure 4. One is of the old self; the other is of the new self. Below these drawings write characteristics and actions pertaining to each, which Paul described in Ephesians 4:22-32.

If you read carefully, you found that lust, deceit, falsehood, stealing, filthy talk, unwholesome words, bitterness, wrath, anger, clamor, slander, and malice are characteristics of the old self. You also found that righteousness, holiness, truth, honest labor, sharing, edifying speech, kindness, tenderheartedness, and forgiveness are characteristics of the new self.

As you see, many old patterns of conduct give way to new ones. Kindness replaces bitterness; tenderheartedness replaces hardheartedness; forgiveness replaces slander (Eph. 4:31-32). While Adam's child collects values like germs off the street, verse 20 says, "But you did not learn Christ in this way." Putting together your Christian value system is a deliberate, intentional activity. As your journey continues, determine to rid yourself of the time bombs! And strive to let Christ make your new self your only self!

Old self   New Self

_____   _____

_____   _____

_____   _____

Figure 4

Day 3

TAKING CONTROL

Read Ephesians 5:1-21.

As you read this passage, consider the deliberate, intentional way you are to take control of the uncontrolled in your life.

As you read Ephesians 5:1-21, did you get the feeling that each value of life must be deliberately selected, that no values should be collected without thought? That's right! The old values were collected at random, like germs off the street. The new ones, however, are to be intentionally selected. Where are these new values to be found? The answer is in Ephesians 5:1.

When revising your personal value system, the most important thing you require is a model to copy. Ephesians 5:1 provides that model for you: "Be imitators of God, as beloved children." Does that overwhelm you? How can you be an imitator of God? Don't overlook the explanation: "as beloved children." Let's take a look at what that means.

Three-year-old Jimmy is standing in the bathroom, watching his daddy shave. The foam, the razor, and the process of removing the beard fascinate him. Later that day his mother suddenly realizes everything is a bit too quiet! She calls out, "Jimmy, where are you?" There is a slight noise in the bath-

When revising your personal value system, the most important thing you require is a model to copy.

13

room, which causes her to move quickly. As she enters, she sees Jimmy on a chair, with foam over his face, his ears, and even in his hair. In his hand is a toy razor given to him for his birthday; he is just starting to "shave."

Jimmy is an "imitator of his daddy, as a beloved child." Whatever his daddy does, he wants to do! Nothing is more important to him than growing up to be like his dad. He talks like him, practices walking like him, even uses the same language he uses. You see, his daddy is his model. This lad is never overwhelmed by the fact that his daddy is older, taller, wiser, stronger, and actually has whiskers. Instead, he believes that one day he is going to be like his daddy. He never thinks that it might be impossible. Instead, he is controlled by his desire to be like his dad.

At the same time, Jimmy's daddy loves Jimmy very much. Because of that deep love his daddy hopes his beloved son will imitate his traits. As you take control of the uncontrolled, imitate God. He is your Model, and He loves you deeply.

Ephesians 5:3-18 spells out some of the old trash that you may need to clean out of your treasure chest. The list of things to be tossed out is amazing! How could anyone place value on immorality, impurity, greed, filthy and silly talk, dirty jokes, covetousness, and idol worship (vv. 3-5)? When non-Christian models are copied, these things actually seem to have worth.

Now that you're a Christian, think back on the persons you have intentionally copied throughout your life. Which ones were not worthy models? List several at the top of the next column.

_____

_____

List characteristics that made these persons seem like good models at the time but now seem to be unworthy of a Christian.

_____

_____

Are any of the characteristics you named listed in Ephesians 5:1-21? If so, circle them. You'll probably see that the unworthy habits of life have changed very little, if at all, since Paul wrote this letter.

You don't have to look to fallible human beings anymore for your ultimate spiritual model. You have a perfect model: God Himself! Now you can "walk as children of light" (v. 8).

Notice the suggestion in verse 10 that you try "to learn what is pleasing to the Lord." Your deliberate, intentional acts will make the difference in your life's values. Remember what we learned on day 1: you deliberately select every value in your life. No one does it for you. This is also true about the new life you have in Christ. The deliberate, intentional addition of Christian values and the rejection of evil values are conscious activities in which you must actively engage.

You may be asking yourself: But how can I learn what is pleasing to God? I want to imitate Him, but how do I know what

He's like? These are legitimate questions. Maybe some of the following suggestions will help.

Read the following list and place a check mark beside those you think would help you learn more about God and His will for you.
❑ Watch a lot of television.
❑ Read books by reliable Christian authors.
❑ Study the Bible by myself and with a group.
❑ Attend worship in my church.
❑ Participate in my church's discipleship activities.
❑ Spend time with God in a daily quiet time.
❑ Cultivate friendships with other Christians.

You should have checked all of the suggestions except the first one. Watching a lot of television will probably not give you much information about God's will. In fact, it may even distract you from more worthy activities. To stress the importance of taking control of uncontrolled values, Paul quoted from a hymn the early Christians sang:

"Awake, sleeper,
And arise from the dead,
And Christ will shine on you" (Eph. 5:14).

Those old values, absorbed like germs from the street, should be examined by a wide-awake you! Intentionally and actively seeking to know the Lord's will should be a characteristic of your life. There's no room for any value that did not come from studying the Model, your new Father.

You are well into your first week. Are you taking time to read your Bible and pray? Are you working on your Scripture-memory verses? Scripture memorization is an important part of your study.

Day 4

survival is a choice

Read 1 Peter 5:8-10 and Ephesians 6:10-18.

He was thin, tattooed, and tough. As he sat on Saint John's Island, looking over the water toward the tall buildings of Singapore, he recalled the Death March he had survived. During World War II he was trapped on that city-island when the Japanese invaded and the British fled. Taken prisoner, he and thousands of others became slave laborers. Their assignment was to build a railroad from Singapore to Bangkok for their captors. Into the malaria-ridden swamps of Malaysia the men went, working until disease and exposure began to take their toll of life. The men were given barely enough rice to survive, and they soon began to look like the living dead.

"As dozens of men began to die all around me," he said, "I knew I had to make a decision. Stronger men than I were just

There's no room for any value that did not come from studying the Model, your new Father.

giving up and dying. Leaning on a shovel, watching a Japanese soldier shoot a man so weak with dysentery that he could no longer work, I determined that I would live through the ordeal. When we were finally freed by Allied troops, I was one of only a few hundred who remained."

Satan will do everything he can to destroy your effectiveness as a Christian, the joy of fellowship and service, and your relationship with the Father. The Bible warns, "Your adversary, the devil, prowls about like a roaring lion, seeking someone to devour" (1 Pet. 5:8). You must be alert to your enemy and make a deliberate, conscious decision that you will survive in spite of his efforts to destroy you.

The old values Satan encouraged you to select before you became a Christian are still hanging on, and Satan will use these as his entry points into your life. That is why they must be tossed out. Each one you allow to remain unchallenged gives Satan a secret tunnel into the center of your existence.

Satan uses at least three entry points to tunnel into your life. The first of these is your emotions, feelings, and desires. This area of life is probably the most difficult to challenge and to change. Things like anger, hatred, envy, lust, greed, and fear can lie hidden and then spring forth in your life so easily and quickly that they become easy entry points for Satan.

Another entry point Satan will try to use is the habits and patterns of your old lifestyle. In Ephesians 2 Paul reminded the Ephesian Christians of their old lifestyle (vv. 1-3). Then he reminded them that God, in His grace, had saved them and had recreated them for a new lifestyle (v. 10). Christians who are determined to survive must constantly guard against the temptation to slip back into the old lifestyle. Values related to the old lifestyle must be challenged and must be cast out, or Satan will use them as easy entry points back into your life.

The third entry point Satan will use is your mind. Some of the understandings, perceptions, assumptions, and judgments you held before you became a Christian were based on incorrect, incomplete, or misinterpreted information. Paul explained to the Christians at Corinth that some of the most crucial issues of life cannot be completely understood or perfectly discerned by persons whose minds are not directed by the Spirit of God. Unless you are willing to allow God to refine some of your old understandings and perceptions and to replace others completely, you are leaving Satan another entry point into your life.

Look at your life right now. Is there one area in which your values are still predominantly unchristian? Maybe in your family relationships or in your business dealings? What about your sexual behavior—is lust or infidelity a problem? You know your values and weak points. List the values you currently have that Satan might use to gain a stronghold in your life.

_____

_____

_____

_____

You can survive, and God has provided you resources to help you survive. In Ephesians 6 Paul listed these resources and compared them to the equipment soldiers wore in that day.

Read Ephesians 6:14-17 and label each part of equipment on the drawing of the soldiers in figure 5. List what each piece is and identify what function you think that piece of equipment serves in your spiritual armor.

Figure 5

Did you notice that there are five defensive weapons (for protection alone) and only one offensive weapon? Name the one part of the armor that can be used to attack as well as to defend.

_____

That's right! The sword! And the sword represents God's Word, the Bible. So what does that tell you about the importance of Bible study and memorization?

_____

_____

_____

Christians can use the Bible to arm themselves against the devil's attacks. When temptation comes, if you're skillful in the use of your sword, God's Word, you can successfully fight it off. That's why it's so important for you to memorize Scripture. If it's in your heart and head, it's always there when you need it.

The man who decided to survive the Japanese death march made a decision to survive as a human being. The choice you make is far more significant: it is a deliberate, willful choice to live as a Christian. If you are to survive, you must develop a survival mentality. Recognize the enemy's desire to devour you, and do not allow him any opportunity to do so. There is no question that your new nature requires new values.

Christians can use the Bible to arm themselves against the devil's attacks.

DON'T DELAY

Read Acts 20:24,27-34.

Paul was facing the toughest period of his whole life. Ahead of him would be "bonds and afflictions." The Spirit of God warned him of these future conditions. It made no difference to Paul! He had sorted through his values. He had tossed out selfishness and empty conceit. He no longer looked out for his own personal interests. He had chosen to follow the One who became obedient to the point of death on a cross. The values formerly collected like germs off the street had been replaced by those of his new life.

The leaders of the church in Ephesus had come to meet Paul at Miletus and had warned him of the coming danger. His unshakable courage is seen in verse 24. Notice what he did not treasure: his own life. He saw little value in seeking to preserve it. Notice what he did treasure: " 'the ministry which I received from the Lord Jesus, to testify solemnly of the gospel of the grace of God.' "

You are a minister! God has given you a ministry just as certainly as He gave Paul a ministry. With a new set of values shaped by the Holy Spirit, you will value your ministry as Paul valued his.

Many Christians have the attitude one young man expressed when he said to a pastor of a vital, committed congregation: "I do not plan to become a member of this church. I would feel obligated to be heavily involved. I would stick out like a sore thumb if I didn't. There are weekends when I prefer to stay away from church, and I would feel guilty doing that. I plan to join another church where I will not have to worry about the reaction if I am absent for a few Sundays."

Paul would have had no part of such shallow values! To him his ministry was his life. He had no desire to take vacations from being a minister. It's all well and good to talk about commitment, but the real proof is in your actions. How did Paul show in a concrete, easily understood way that his commitment to God's work was complete?

Read Acts 20:27,31. Write the two things Paul did that showed his commitment. Paul showed his commitment by:

1. _____

2. _____

What commitments could you make in your life comparable to the ones Paul made in verse 27 and 31? Write two.

_____

_____

Paul told the elders of the church in Ephesus that he " 'did not shrink from declaring to [them] the whole purpose of God' "

(v. 27). And he added, " 'Night and day for a period of three years I did not cease to admonish each one with tears' " (v. 31). Paul's committed, unceasing work as a minister had established many men and women in their faith.

Yet Paul realized that some persons in the church did not feel a strong commitment to ministry. In verse 30 he warned of persons in the church who would draw a following to feed their egos. Sadly, he recognized that not all of God's children have sorted through their treasure chests, abandoning old values.

As a new Christian, be warned by Paul's words in this passage. Be alerted by your observation of older believers who surprise and disappoint you. Above all, be determined not to follow in their footsteps! Nothing is more dangerous than Christians who are only halfhearted in their walk and who shrink from the call of our Lord to be ministers. Such persons contradict the Christian message. How can one contain the Spirit of Christ, who became obedient to the point of death, yet display values that are self-centered and self-serving?

Have you acknowledged the inevitable commitment your new life in Christ demands of you? Have there already been times when you have had to choose between your own desires and God's will for you? Briefly describe a recent incident when this happened. What did you do? How did you resolve the conflict? How did you feel after you made your decision?

_____

_____

_____

In the committed Christian life old values are replaced by new ones. You are no longer to consider your personal interests. Rather, you are to seek to live for the interests of others. You will not function from selfishness or empty conceit. Instead, your actions will show that you value others just as highly as you value yourself.

Such a lifestyle is the normal Christian lifestyle, not optional for a Christian. You will forsake business as usual to become involved in God's unusual business. You will cherish the ministry He has given you more than you cherish anything else. Make the decision now to enter your ministry, to enter servanthood. Do not delay doing so.

Before you move on to the next part of the journey, take time to recall this week's Scripture-memory verses. Write them from memory.

_____

_____

_____

Don't forget to continue your daily quiet time over the weekend even though you won't be using *Living Your Christian Values*. Instead, use other devotional, Bible-study, or discipleship materials. See you next week!

Nothing is more dangerous than Christians who are only halfhearted in their walk.

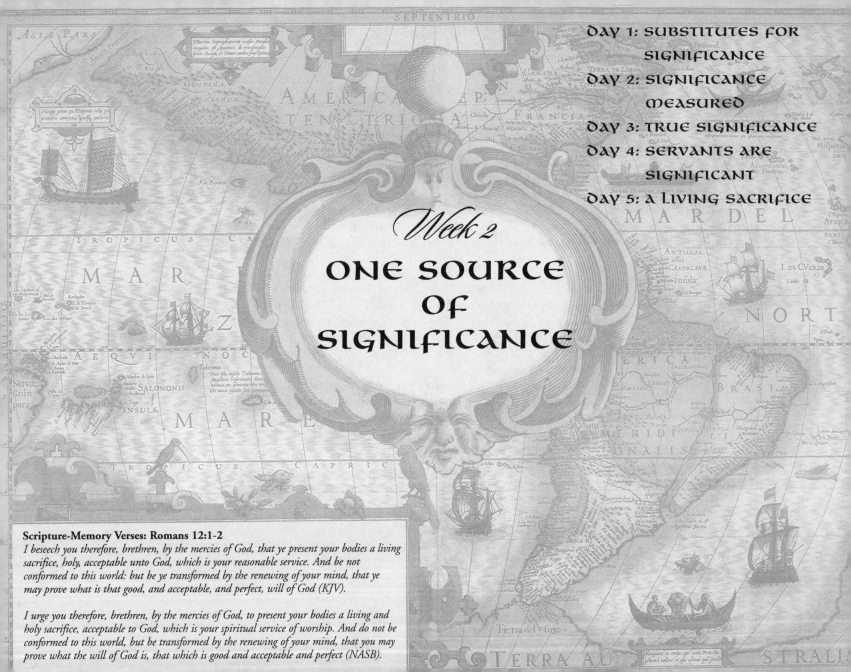

Week 2

ONE SOURCE OF SIGNIFICANCE

Scripture-Memory Verses: Romans 12:1-2
I beseech you therefore, brethren, by the mercies of God, that ye present your bodies a living sacrifice, holy, acceptable unto God, which is your reasonable service. And be not conformed to this world: but be ye transformed by the renewing of your mind, that ye may prove what is that good, and acceptable, and perfect, will of God (KJV).

I urge you therefore, brethren, by the mercies of God, to present your bodies a living and holy sacrifice, acceptable to God, which is your spiritual service of worship. And do not be conformed to this world, but be transformed by the renewing of your mind, that you may prove what the will of God is, that which is good and acceptable and perfect (NASB).

SUBSTITUTES FOR SIGNIFICANCE

Use your Scripture-memory card to begin memorizing Romans 12:1-2.

From the beginning Adam and Eve were the most significant of all created beings. They did not have to become significant; their relationship with God made them significant.

Read Genesis 1:27. Why do human beings have special significance to God?

_____

_____

God created us in His own image. This means that human beings are different from the other creatures God made because God made us like Him.

List characteristics we share with God, our Heavenly Father.

_____

_____

_____

You may have mentioned that we are spiritual beings as well as physical beings. God is also a spiritual being. We have the ability to create just as God creates. We have the capacity to love just as God loves. This ability to love and to have fellowship demonstrates the significance of every human being.

Read Genesis 3:1-6,16-19.

As far as we know, neither Adam nor Eve had given any serious thought to the privileges they had as the specially loved children of God. Then Satan spoke to Eve and planted a value in her mind. Could she not be significant for her own accomplishments rather than just because of her relationship with the Father? The value Satan used to lure Eve was the possibility of being " 'like God, knowing good and evil' " (Gen. 3:5). That appealed to her! She saw "that the tree was desirable to make one wise" (Gen. 3:6). Deep within her was a determination to become significant through her accomplishments rather than because of her relationship with the Father. Adam was quick to follow her. He too desired to become renowned for what he did rather than because he was special to God. Adam and Eve made a value decision that has been repeated by every person. We all have the urge to earn significance.

What did this decision cost Adam and Eve? It cost them the garden and all of its blessings. Worst of all, it cost them their relationship with the Father. What did they gain? They "gained" the fully developed desire to be significant as a result of their accomplishments. Eve "gained" great pain in childbirth, and Adam "gained" thorns and thistles in the ground he was to till. They "gained" a competitive spirit and with it jealousy and envy.

The ability to love and to have fellowship demonstrates the significance of every human being.

Even Christians feel this inherited urge to "be somebody" because of their own accomplishments. Think about your life. What drives and ambitions make you feel significant? Do certain achievements make you feel important? List them under the heading *Ambitions* in figure 6.

Take a look at the ambitions you listed. What did the fulfillment of these ambitions cost you? Write under *Cost* on the chart what you had to give up to obtain your goal.

Let's analyze your feelings even further. What did you actually gain from achieving your ambition? Was it worth the cost? Was it what you expected? Describe under *Gain* on the chart the results of achieving your goal.
After looking over your chart, can you draw any conclusions about the desire to make yourself into a "somebody" by your accomplishments? Summarize your insights.

_____

_____

The children of Adam feel that the primary value of life is to earn their worth—to become a "somebody." Each person wants to make a mark on the world. This value enslaves people. They are no longer free to be who God made them to be. Significance is always a goal that is never achieved. No matter how much a person achieves, no matter how much money he earns, no matter how much power he gains, it is never quite enough. If we base our worth on achievement, we will always feel empty and disappointed.

The Bible reports of men who tried to earn significance through their accomplishments. Read Genesis 4:16-25.

After killing his brother because he felt his own significance was being overshadowed, Cain "went out from the presence of the Lord" (v. 16) and built a city. Lamech was one of the first men to take more than one wife. Jabal, Lamech's son, became the first nomad. Jabal's brother, Jubal, became renowned as a musician, playing the lyre and the pipe. Another son, Tubal-cain, became the world's first industrialist, forging implements of bronze and iron. Each found a way to be recognized.

Figure 6

Ambitions	Cost	Gain
_____	_____	_____
_____	_____	_____
_____	_____	_____

Tragically, Lamech illustrates the end that comes of those who spend their lives seeking fame and fortune. Blind and arrogant in his self-worth and imagined power, Lamech vowed to cut down those who stood in his way or who posed a threat to him. Then the scriptural account simply turns from Lamech and his descendants. The silence that remains seems to thunder that there is no future, nothing worth remembering, nothing of significance in God's eyes for persons who live life apart from Him. Cattle, music, industry, and building cities all occupied the life spans of these men, but not one of them found true significance through his accomplishments.

Identify the types of achievements you see people today pursuing to gain self-worth.

_____

_____

_____

You may have identified any number of pursuits, such as s*ports, cooking, education, politics, wealth, power,* and *pleasure.* Yet running parallel to all of these inner drives, misery exists within each person. The treasure chests of values are filled with "street germs." A marriage falls apart. A business goes bankrupt. Some turn to drugs. Emptiness exists within.

In Ecclesiastes 6 the wisest of Israel's kings reflected on such people. Read that chapter.

"All a man's labor is for his mouth and yet the appetite is not satisfied" (v. 7). That is the story of persons apart from God. If they do something well, they feel worthy. If they do something poorly, they feel worthless. Life is a series of strivings to be important, and nothing brings final, total satisfaction.

There is a problem with basing your self-worth and significance on your accomplishments. Write one reason why you can never be ultimately satisfied with this striving.

_____

_____

_____

The answer is eloquently stated in Ecclesiastes 6:12: "Who knows what is good for a man during his lifetime, during the few years of his futile life? He will spend them like a shadow. For who can tell a man what will be after him under the sun?" We can never be good enough to satisfy ourselves. Failure is a part of the human condition.

Adam's race has not realized there is an entirely different way to live: a way of happiness, based on a relationship with the Father. What can ever match the great worth of becoming a child of God? As Cowboy Joe Evans used to say, "If God has called you to be His child, don't ever stoop to become kings or presidents." Any human position of honor is a step below the significance of belonging to the Heavenly Father!

Any human position of honor is a step below the significance of belonging to the Heavenly Father!

Day 2

SIGNIFICANCE MEASURED

Adam had another problem! Read Psalm 12:1-4.

Having rejected the source of his true significance, his personal relationship with God, Adam would now have to find his affirmation in another source. The same is true of Adam's children today. Those who seek to be significant through their achievements must have special people to affirm them. Throughout history, people have classified one another as significant and insignificant. Those to impress are those of your own "class." Those in "less important classes" do not matter, and those in the "more important classes" are probably unimpressed by your accomplishments.

Therefore, all of us learn to play by the rules of Adam's game at an early age. We first select something to do to make us significant, and then we select the class of people who will admire us. Clubs, organizations, trophies, plaques, medals, awards all grow from our wish to be admired for our accomplishments.

When "the godly man ceases to be" (v. 1), he must turn to a source other than God to be admired. Along with the end of the godly man comes the end of the faithful man (v. 1). The psalmist was under no illusions about people! He said, "They speak falsehood [emptiness] to one another; with flattering lips and with a double heart they speak" (v. 2). Verse 4 testifies to the empty words, flattery, and doubleheartedness that reign in a world where people seek to impress and gain recognition.

From your study so far, state the two biggest values in Adam's treasure chest.

1. _____

2. _____

You may have listed: *(1) the determination to be significant and (2) the need to have special people around to flatter him and to speak great things about him.* These are still the primary values in the treasure chests of Adam's children.

Adam's children are not free to be what God created them to be, because they have selected lesser goals for life. Since those goals cannot ever be fully reached, life is always lived in frustration. No honor is ever enough. They can never relax because there is always a higher mountain to climb.

The stubborn rejection of God's desire to adopt Adam's children and give them significance is described in Psalm 12:4. They say: " 'With our tongue we will prevail; our lips are our own; who is lord over us?' " Who indeed? Those two huge values in the treasure chest reign as lord over them. Freedom is only an illusion.

When you entered God's family, you left behind the need for significance and the need for other people to affirm it. Even more than Adam was, you are God's child. You have constant fellowship with Him. You have no need for "class" consciousness. All are equally loved by God, and all can be equally loved by you!

Is it hard for you to accept that you don't have to do anything to be significant in God's eyes? Everything in our upbringing and in our society teaches us that we aren't important unless we do something or have something. But once you became a Christian and you entered a personal relationship with God, you gained a freedom to be who God created you to be. Now you can accept yourself just the way you are—warts and all! And not only yourself but others, too.

Although you may need to experience growth and change in your life, you do not have to do so to earn God's love and acceptance. God loves you just the way you are.

Beside figure 7 write: *Sure, I'm not perfect, but God loves and accepts me just the way I am.*

Is there a connection between the values stored in your treasure chest and your personal feeling of worth? Yes! Paul's comments about the way he lived as a child of Adam explain this.

Read Philippians 3:4-7.

In verse 4 Paul explained that he had previously placed his confidence "in the flesh." What did he mean? His self-confidence came from what his flesh had accomplished, not from what the Spirit of God had done in him.

In verses 5 and 6 Paul outlined the former measurements of his significance:
- "Circumcised the eighth day." As a Jew, it was important to Paul to be a child of Abraham's covenant.
- "Of the nation of Israel, of the tribe of Benjamin, a Hebrew of Hebrews." Paul was no run-of-the-mill Jew. He was a part of the finest and most respected community of Jews, and he was proud of it.

God loves you just the way you are.

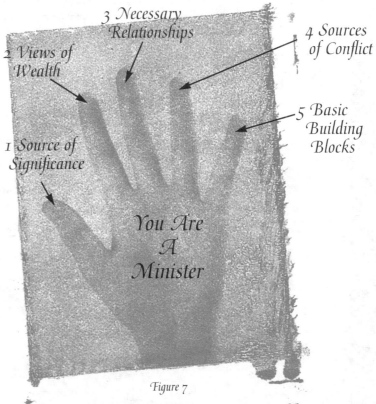

3 Necessary Relationships

4 Sources of Conflict

2 Views of Wealth

5 Basic Building Blocks

1 Source of Significance

You Are A Minister

Figure 7

• "As to the Law, a Pharisee." More than just a religious title, becoming a Pharisee involved breeding, education, status, and power. Paul considered himself to be politically and socially important.
• "As to zeal, a persecutor of the church." Paul's worth partially resulted from the intensity of his activity as a Pharisee. He was ambitious for honor and took on the most difficult tasks to get it.
• "As to the righteousness which is in the Law, found blameless." Excelling above others made Paul feel significant. Others might cut corners in their religious piety, but Paul would not. He was proud of his rigid lifestyle.

Paul's list of "right" religious activities could be duplicated and translated for today. Some believe that the right background, religious affiliations, and religious activities make them superior to the rest of humanity. The following activity will help you compare Paul's list of accomplishments in Philippians 3:5-6 to accomplishments people might boast about today.

Match Paul's religious accomplishment (1.-5.) with a comparable modern-day accomplishment (a.-e.).

___ 1. Circumcised on the eighth day
___ 2. Of the nation of Israel, of the tribe of Benjamin
___ 3. A Pharisee
___ 4. Obeyed every commandment of the law

a. A loyal church member
b. Leads an exemplary life in the community
c. Baptized as a nine year old
d. Born into a good Christian family

You probably answered this way: *1. c, 2. d, 3. a, 4. b.* Even though all but one on the list of modern-day religious activities is good and commendable, none is a substitute for a personal relationship with God. Just as Paul's works of the flesh were meaningless without a real love for God, our own "righteous" church behavior is empty unless we abide in God's love. Paul's status as a Jew, education, title, activity, and self-discipline had once made him significant in his own eyes. Notice that most of the values Paul used to describe himself were "decent" things. Even when combined, they did not seem terribly evil. That was precisely what made them so dangerous! None of them revealed the cold, unfeeling person who had created them as a way of measuring his importance. He was callused to the needs of others. He thought only of his own status, his own fame.

A single event completely changed Paul's old ways of measuring his value. The old ways were no longer valid: "Whatever things were gain to me, those things I have counted as loss for the sake of Christ" (v. 7). He cleaned out his treasure chest.

In a quiet time with God, ask Him to reveal values that may seem righteous and worthy to you but in fact may cause pain for others. If the Holy Spirit reveals a value in your treasure chest that needs to be thrown out, write it on the trash can in figure 8. This visually depicts what Paul said in Philippians 3:8: "More than that, I count all things to be loss in view of the surpassing value of knowing Christ Jesus my Lord, for whom I have suffered the loss of all things, and count them but rubbish in order that I may gain Christ."

Day 3

TRUE SIGNIFICANCE

The problem with treasure chests is that they are temporary! Read Ecclesiastes 2:11-26.

Born as Adam's child, you carefully sorted through objects, pleasures, and people, storing away values that seemed to have worth. Then, as an adult, you began to live inside your treasure chest, still seeking the greatest treasure of all: the meaning of life. One day, perhaps without warning, death will come. Will life have been meaningful?

A person who was not a Christian was asked, "What is the purpose of life?" He replied: "That question baffles me. I don't really know what my purpose is or why I am here. But as long as I'm here, I'm going to enjoy myself; that's all I know." His answer was typical. His values snugly wrapped around him as he talked, insulating him from the awareness that death will end everything for him. His only purpose for living was to enjoy himself. A household pet could say the same thing!

Before you became a Christian, did you ever wonder, *What is the meaning of life?* Did you look around at the suffering, the poverty, and the evil in the world and wonder, *What is my role in all this?* Most people have asked these questions at some

point in their lives. As Adam's child, you may not have had a satisfactory answer. But as God's child, you have an answer!

Read Ephesians 5:1-2. As a Christian, what is your purpose in life? (Here's a clue: The answer is expressed as two commands.) Write your answer.

1. _____

2. _____

Figure 8

As the Scripture passage expresses, a Christian's purpose in life is (1) to be an imitator of his Heavenly Father and (2) to walk in love. Ecclesiastes describes the best people can do when they choose to live without God. Many verses in Ecclesiastes describe the emptiness of a faithless life. Life apart from God is always without profit. Solomon asked, "What does a man get in all his labor and in his striving with which he labors under the sun?" (Eccl. 2:22). His answer is cynical: "Thus I considered all my activities which my hands had done and the labor which I had exerted, and behold all was vanity [futility] and striving after wind and there was no profit under the sun" (Eccl. 2:11). For Solomon, life without God was like an empty bubble that grew bigger and bigger. The end of existence was the bubble's bursting. Nothing remained. But what of the activities men selected to make themselves significant? Do they remain? No! They also vanish when the bubble bursts.

Solomon valued wisdom, and he gained significance as the wisest man in the world. When he evaluated all of the years devoted to wisdom, he concluded that "wisdom excels folly as light excels darkness" (Eccl. 2:13). But what will death, the

As a Christian, what is your purpose in life?

great leveler, do to the values of the wise man and the fool? Solomon saw that one fate, death, will claim them both. He said to himself: " 'As is the fate of the fool, it will also befall me. Why then have I been extremely wise?' " (Eccl. 2:15).

He looked at his bubble, about to burst, and continued: " 'This too is vanity [futility].' For there is no lasting remembrance of the wise man as with the fool, inasmuch as in the coming days all will be forgotten. And how the wise man and the fool alike die! So I hated life, for the work which had been done under the sun was grievous to me; because everything is futility and striving after wind" (Eccl. 2:15-17).

Because you have been adopted into the Father's royal priesthood, life is not like that for you! Solomon wrote in Ecclesiastes 2:25, "Who can eat and who can have enjoyment without Him?" Becoming a child of the King opened up eternity for you; life no longer has death as a terminal point. Above all, you have learned that your life has meaning and purpose. You are a minister. You live each precious hour of your life on a different level from that of Adam's children. You need not search for a special activity that will impress others with your importance. Nor do you require the special people who will flatter you and make you feel that you have worth.

You are a child of the King! That fact in itself is so significant that nothing you will ever do can make you more significant. Unlike other people, you could become the best without concern for how important it makes you look to others. Excelling at something will point to the majesty of the One who created your capacities and will glorify His name, not yours.

For you, there is no bursting bubble. There are no treasured values by which you will prove to the world that you are significant. There is, instead, a relationship. You have a Father, and you are His child. You are free to enjoy Him not only for the rest of your life but forever!

As you have learned, your way of deciding your value as a person was shaped long before you became God's child. You programmed yourself over a long period of time to measure your worth by what others think of you.

What are criteria by which you have measured your self-worth in the past? List some.

_____

_____

In the past you may have relied on standards like your looks or your ability to make money for your self-worth. It's time to throw out old, false values and adopt a new one, a Christian one: God created you in His image. As His adopted one, you are made to be like Him. Your life reflects God's character; you exhibit His glory.

Read Matthew 18:1-6. Adam's children seek to be significant by their achievements; the children of God are significant simply because …

_____

_____

God's children are significant simply because they are God's children. Consider the value system in a child's treasure chest. Does a three-year old become significant by performing a great feat, by collecting great wealth, or by attaining great knowledge? No, the child is not capable of great feats. Does the child have an inner, driving urge to become significant by doing something impressive? No! A child is content just to be, without any fear of being considered worthless. The child has security and peace and calm because he is loved for who he is and not what he has done. Jesus said, " 'Unless you are converted [changed] and become like children, you shall not enter the kingdom of heaven' " (Matt. 18:3).

What particular childlike characteristics should you strive to have in your life? Circle the characteristics you should develop as a child of God.

trusting	fearful	dependent	honest
secure	willful	obedient	self-centered
loving	teachable		

Children of loving parents are usually trusting, dependent, honest, secure, obedient, loving, and teachable. These are traits you should seek to possess, too.

When you became a child of God, His Spirit entered your life. He is continually shaping your conduct, your mind, your emotions. You must be significant to receive such attention from God! God loves you deeply. You need only be His child to please Him. He accepts you totally. You do not have to merit His favor by doing a great deed for Him. Instead, simply reveal His indwelling life within you. Others' critical or flattering words do not subtract from or add to your significance. The basis of your significance is a relationship!

When Christ is your Lord, you are free to become the servant of all. Instead of spending your life becoming important, you can bring meaning to others by serving them. You can afford to lose your life in caring, giving, and loving. You can risk being vulnerable rather than protecting yourself all the time.

Read the following Scripture verses and check the one that best summarizes the concept being discussed.

❑ Matthew 9:37   ❑ Matthew 24:13   ❑ Matthew 16:25

Did you recognize Matthew 16:25? " 'Whoever wishes to save his life shall lose it; but whoever loses his life for My sake shall find it.' " When you're a child of God, you've already gained your life—now and for eternity. So you can afford to give your life away in service to others!

To be totally free, each person must make two choices. The first, as you learned today, is to become a child of God. The second deliberate choice is to toss out of the treasure chest the determination to be first and to replace it with a desire to become a servant of all; that's tomorrow's topic.

Does being a servant mean that you give up the desire to do great things? Of course not! But the motive for your performance will be entirely different. Instead of seeking to gain significance by what you do, excelling in an area is the result of showing forth God's creative power in you. All the glory will go to Him. Simply being His child makes you significant!

The basis of your significance is a relationship!

Are you learning this week's Scripture-memory verses? Try writing them here from memory.

_____

_____

_____

Day 4

SERVANTS ARE SIGNIFICANT

Can you recall from yesterday's lesson the two choices you must make to be totally free?

1. _____

2. _____

The two choices are: *(1) to become a child of God* and *(2) to become a servant of all.* Yesterday you learned the significance of being a child of God. Today you will learn the significance of being His servant.

Read Mark 9:33-37.

Jesus and the disciples had just come to Capernaum. On the trip the disciples had been whispering among themselves. Which one would become the greatest among them? Jesus knew that their value system had to be changed. It was time to teach them about God's way of valuing people.

Jesus explained God's value system in one simple statement. Reread Mark 9:35; write that statement here.

_____

_____

Jesus' value system was amazingly simple but amazingly surprising: " 'If anyone wants to be first, he shall be last of all, and servant of all.' " Jesus' words seem to be the direct opposite of what we typically think, don't they? What opposites do you see in this radical and life-changing concept of greatness? Fill in the blanks.

To be first, you must be _____.

To be great, you must be _____ of all.

It's hard to believe that to be first, you must be last; that to be great, you must be the servant of all. What does it mean to be the servant of all? First, such a person has no need to be important. Servants do not use their energy to attain great feats, great wealth, or great knowledge. Servants are ministers, responding to others' needs. Decisions about what they will do are made by their masters. Servants own nothing; instead, they take care of their masters' possessions.

In addition, a servant is totally free from the need to gain recognition by doing something to become significant. Servants, in this sense, are the only free people. All others are slaves to their desire for importance. Released from that desire, servants have an inner peace. For them, serving others as directed by the master is enough to give meaning to life.

Do you see another seemingly opposite statement here? Read the following statements; then fill in the blanks.

Servants, or slaves, are the only _____ people. All others are _____ to their desire to be important.

That's right. According to God's way of looking at reality (which is now your way too since you are His child), to be free, you must be a slave. And if you try to be free, apart from committing yourself totally to God, you will be a slave to your own desires! Another true opposite!

Mark 9:36-37 records that Jesus used a small child to illustrate His point about servanthood. Why would Jesus select a child for His object lesson? Jesus said: " 'Whoever receives one child like this in My name receives Me' " (v. 37). The word *receive* mean*s to take with the hand; not to refuse friendship.*

Jesus was saying that His disciples must have the kind of attitude that would not prevent their being servants to this child. Such an assignment was beneath their dignity because they aspired to be great! Slaves assigned to baby-sit small children were the least in status, even among slaves. Our Lord was saying, "Serving such a child, as degrading as it seems in your eyes, is equal to serving Me, and whoever does so is minister-

ing not only to Me but also to Him who sent Me." God's value system meant they must become the servant of all—even persons they may have considered insignificant.

As the time for His crucifixion drew near, Jesus used a dramatic method to teach His disciples the significance of servanthood. Read John 12:25-26 and 13:1-17.

Twelve men in an upper room had one thing on their minds: significance! They expected to gain respect by becoming powerful men. "Soon," they whispered to one another, "Jesus will overthrow the Romans and take control of Israel." Then they would come into their positions of status in His new empire.

There were thousands of slaves in the Roman Empire. None of the twelve were of that despised class! Not one of the twelve had considered accepting the role of a slave. Consequently, the towel and basin by the door, used only by a slave assigned to wash the feet of free men, remained untouched. There had always been small inconveniences, like not having a slave to wash their feet. Soon they would be compensated. Soon Jesus would make His move.

Jesus' heart ached as He observed the twelve! Believing they were free men, they were actually slaves to their need to be significant. His words recorded in John 12:25-26 had made no impact. He knew they would never be truly free until they rid their treasure chests of the need for status.

Status may be defined as *position or rank in relation to others; as relative rank in a hierarchy of prestige.* Did you notice the words *relation* and *relative* in these definitions? They emphasize the

If you try to be free, apart from committing yourself totally to God, you will be a slave to your own desires!

fact that status is a measure of how you stack up against others. It is a comparative state of being.

Why do Adam's children place a high value on their status?

_____

And why should you, as God's child, not worry about your status in the eyes of others?

_____

You probably mentioned that Adam's children depend on other persons to evaluate their worth. Therefore, their status is an important measure to them. But once you become God's child, the only measure of your worth is your relationship with Him. Your rank in a human hierarchy is no longer important.

Jesus wanted to convey this idea to His disciples, but His opportunities to teach were drawing to a close. Time remained for only two lessons to be taught! The first would begin now. Jesus stripped to His undergarment and assumed the dress of a slave. He walked to the doorway, took the basin and towel, and began to do the work of a slave. Peter recoiled! He did not want Jesus to wash his feet, for a good reason. He still had not learned the lesson that Jesus had tried to teach the disciples about greatness. After He had washed their feet, Jesus asked, " 'Do you know what I have done to you?' " (John 13:12). They knew He had washed their feet, but they did not understand the value He was trying to teach. Jesus began by pointing to His status: as their Teacher and Lord had served them, they were to serve others. Although others might base their

value on significant accomplishments and on power and position, they were to value serving others. Being a servant was the standard by which they would measure their value.

Think about your life. Are there things that really need to be done, but you have avoided doing them because they seem to be beneath your dignity? Have you neglected to help or serve in certain ways at home or at church because you felt that the job was too menial? Jesus showed us in a graphic way that no job is too menial. Our love for others should make any task seem worthwhile and important.

In figure 9 you see a wash bucket and a sponge. On the bucket write at least three specific things you can do to help someone this week. On the sponge write the reason behind your willingness to be a servant.

Figure 9

The disciples did not understand the lesson Jesus taught them at the Last Supper. But after His second lesson had been taught, they would! During the night they slept; Jesus prayed about the ordeal that would teach the second lesson. Then He saw torches flickering in the valley below Him. The time for the second lesson had arrived. He was led through the streets of Jerusalem on His death march. What "status" did He hold as He walked crowned by thorns, beard ripped out, skin hanging by strips down His back and chest?

Jesus next performed an act of servanthood far beyond that of caring for a small child or washing feet! As nails pierced His hands and feet, the sins of the whole world were laid on Him. The disciples' minds were in turmoil. Had they been wrong? Would He not become king of the Jews? What was happening? Hiding in garrets, the disciples recalled His words: " 'He who loves his life loses it; and he who hates his life in this world shall keep it to life eternal. … and where I am, there shall My servant also be' " (John 12:25-26). Slowly they would understand:

1. You are significant because you are God's child.
2. You are free because you don't prove significance by what you do.
3. Your freedom permits you to become the servant of all.
4. As a servant, you invest your life in meaningful activity for others.
5. Being a minister, no matter how costly, is the highest way to use your life!

Have you seriously committed yourself to servanthood as the greatest of all values in life? Jesus asks you to do so. Give up the game of seeking personal worth by impressive achievements. Let your activities carry out tasks God has assigned to you as a servant-minister. Avoid actions motivated by a desire to gain status and fame. Servanthood is significant. Your Lord delights in it—and in you when you choose this way of life.

a LIVING SACRIFICE

Being a minister, no matter how costly, is the highest way to use your life!

Today you will complete your second week of this study! See if you can remember the subject you have been studying and write it in on the thumb in figure 10.

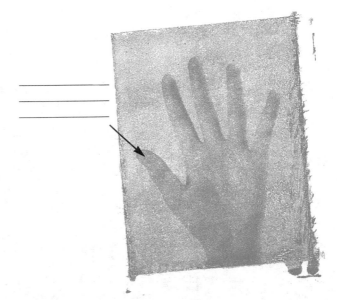

Figure 10

Did you write *One Source of Significance* on the thumb? And what is that source of significance? Write it here.

_____

You probably had no trouble remembering that a Christian's significance is found in his relationship with God.

Before the week is over, ask someone to read along in the Bible as you say Romans 12:1-2 from memory. Then explain the meaning of these verses. That will test your understanding as well as your memory. Whom can you ask to do this for you? Write that person's name here.

_____

Now—on to our study for today!

When you are God's child, you are also His slave. Read Romans 11:33-36 and recall from memory 12:1-2.

The phrase "I urge you therefore" in Romans 12:1 links a command (Rom. 12:1-2) with the reason for that command (Rom. 11:33-36). Recall Romans 12:1 now and write Paul's command.

_____

The command is "Present your bodies a living and holy sacrifice." That is an awesome, overpowering requirement! It calls for you to die in advance of your physical death and then surrender to God the life that still exists as His exclusive possession. To put it another way, it is a command to become His slave, surrendering all personal privileges and possessions. That command is not something to be done by your intellect or your emotions, or even by both combined. It is something to be done with your whole being. Therefore, the command describes a value—the most basic value ever to be placed in your treasure chest: to become a living sacrifice, a slave.

Perhaps you are thinking: *There has to be a good reason for doing something so radical, so final, and so total. Why should I?* The reason, stated in Romans 11:33-36, is even more awesome than the command! Those verses describe God's nature.

As you review Romans 11:33-36, fill in the spaces in the character résumé in figure 11. You will formulate a short, concise description of God's overwhelming nature.

Character Résumé

Name: God, Lord, the Almighty
Job title: Creator and Sustainer of
*   the universe*
Judgments: unsearchable
Ways:
Mind:
Counselor:
Debts:
Relationship to all things:

Figure 11

Now can you see why Paul gave his command? God's matchless character makes Him worthy of your complete devotion. His judgments are unsearchable. His ways are unfathomable. No one knows His mind, and no one is His counselor. He owes no debts to anyone. And everything that exists is from Him, through Him, and to Him!

In light of God's character, how absurd it seems for human beings to strut like peacocks, seeking to accumulate personal worth and fame to impress other humans. They are so insignificant when measured by God!

In Romans 12:1 Paul said that becoming a living sacrifice is a rational act. It makes sense! One's own importance must be kept in perspective. Compare yourself to God—your mind, your capacities, your personal powers, and the strength and integrity of your moral character. The comparison helps settle the issue, doesn't it? God alone is important.

Paul gives a key to the best way to become a living sacrifice. He said in verse 2, "Do not be conformed to this world, but be transformed by the renewing of your mind." What does this mean? Decide which of the following statements is true or false. Write *T* beside true statements and *F* beside false statements.

_____ 1. Being conformed to this world means that the values in your treasure chest are the same as those of Adam's children.

_____ 2. To avoid being conformed to the world, you must totally withdraw from it.

_____ 3. When your mind is renewed by God, your values are transformed, too.

_____ 4. If you have been transformed by God, you will find it natural to make your life a living sacrifice.

Did these statements clarify Romans 12:2? All the statements were true except the second. You don't have to avoid the world if God has renewed and transformed your mind. Rather, you will want to try to work in the world as God's servant.

There is a huge difference between praying, "Lord, please bless what I'm doing" and praying, "Lord, let me do what You're blessing!" In the first prayer you are the master. In the second prayer God is Master. Which prayer do you usually pray? Your honest answer is a good way to test whether you have presented your body as a living sacrifice.

More than a century ago Abraham Kuyper said, "There is not an inch of any sphere of life over which Jesus Christ does not say, 'Mine!' " That includes you. God made you to be a living sacrifice. Paul said, " 'In Him we live and move and exist' " (Acts 17:28). God is the inescapable one. He alone is important! Are you beginning to see why being a servant-minister is significant? No servant has ever existed alone. Whenever you find a servant, you will find a master, and you will find a relationship existing between them.

Take a moment now to tell God that you want to make your life a living sacrifice to Him today and every day.

Read Luke 14:26-27.

Whenever you find a servant, you will find a master, and you will find a relationship existing between them.

Jesus' teaching in Luke 14:26 forever releases you from a dependency on being affirmed by other people. The word hate in verse 26 is to be understood in light of the entire statement. That is, you are not being commanded to hate your relatives literally but rather to love Christ so deeply that, by comparison, your love for your family seems to be hate.

Basing your worth on what others think of you is a perfect way to become permanently miserable. Because your significance rests on your being a child of God and not just the child of your father and mother, everything changes. You become His servant, and your life is committed to being His minister.

Servanthood has no limits. Even dying on a cross as Jesus died is not too radical a thought! When you are a living sacrifice, your greatest value is to use your life in God's service.

When physical life is over, eternal life with Him has just begun. That means your significance as a child of God will last forever. Relationships, even those between relatives and family members, will terminate, but your fellowship with the Father is timeless.

Someone has said that when a person is carrying a cross, three things are true:
1. He is never going back where he came from.
2. He has no further long-range plans.
3. His possessions are meaningless.

What did Jesus say in Luke 14:27 about crosses?

_____

That's right. Each disciple must carry his own cross and follow Jesus. What does it mean to carry your own cross? (Hint: What did Jesus' cross represent for Him?)

_____

Your cross represents a sacrifice. (For Jesus the cross was the ultimate sacrifice.) It represents the depth of your commitment to Christ: you will put His will first, and anything that stands in your way will be given up.

On the drawing of the cross in figure 12, write one thing you have sacrificed since you became a Christian. Thank God that He gave you the strength to do it!

Figure 12

Eternity is much closer than you think! It's important to live your remaining days totally committed to God! Knowing that you have one source of significance and that it is eternal, let's move on now to look at some important Christian values that must be placed in your treasure chest.

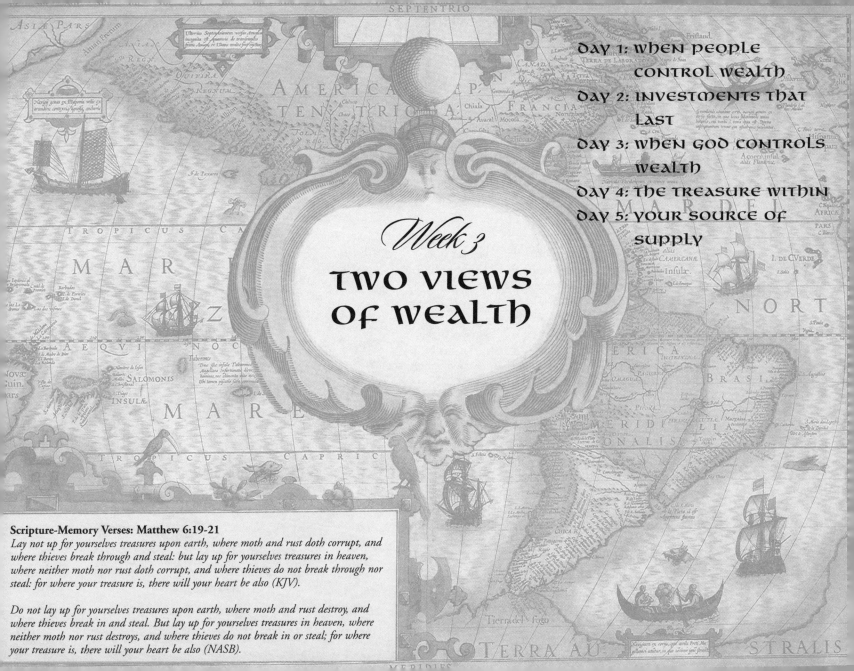

SEPTENTRIO

DAY 1: WHEN PEOPLE
CONTROL WEALTH

DAY 2: INVESTMENTS THAT
LAST

DAY 3: WHEN GOD CONTROLS
WEALTH

DAY 4: THE TREASURE WITHIN

DAY 5: YOUR SOURCE OF
SUPPLY

Week 3

TWO VIEWS
OF WEALTH

Scripture-Memory Verses: Matthew 6:19-21

Lay not up for yourselves treasures upon earth, where moth and rust doth corrupt, and where thieves break through and steal: but lay up for yourselves treasures in heaven, where neither moth nor rust doth corrupt, and where thieves do not break through nor steal: for where your treasure is, there will your heart be also (KJV).

Do not lay up for yourselves treasures upon earth, where moth and rust destroy, and where thieves break in and steal. But lay up for yourselves treasures in heaven, where neither moth nor rust destroys, and where thieves do not break in or steal; for where your treasure is, there will your heart be also (NASB).

when people control wealth

The value of memorizing Scripture cannot be over emphasized. Continue to store God's Word in your mind and heart. Use your Scripture-memory card to begin memorizing Matthew 6:19-21.

Last week you studied the concept of one source of significance. That idea was written on the _____ of the hand diagram. (That's right, the thumb!) Notice what's written on the forefinger in figure 13. This week you'll study two views of wealth.

Read Luke 12:16-19.

Wealth can be viewed in two ways. The first view is that wealth is controlled by persons. What they possess is their property, and they may do with it as they please. The second view, the Christian view, is that wealth is controlled by God. In Luke 12:16-19 we see an example of a man who held the first view. The "certain rich man" betrayed the values stored inside his treasure chest.

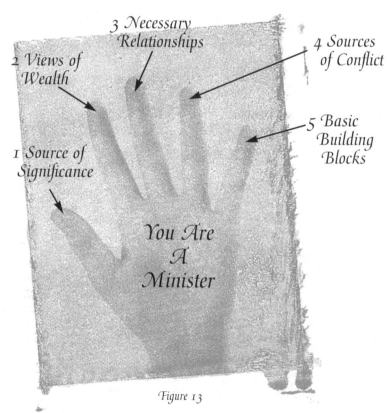

3 *Necessary Relationships*

2 *Views of Wealth*

4 *Sources of Conflict*

5 *Basic Building Blocks*

1 *Source of Significance*

You Are A Minister

Figure 13

Can you identify some of the man's values in Luke 12:16-19? List above the treasure chest below at least three values.

1. _____

2. _____

3. _____

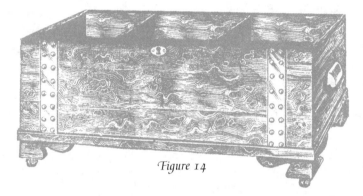

Figure 14

You'll have your own ideas, but you may have found values like *security* (" 'Many goods laid up for many years to come' "); *luxury* (" 'Take your ease' "); *pleasure* (" 'Eat, drink and be merry.' "). You may also have uncovered a fourth value: *independence*. As long as his grain lasted, the rich man needed no one else. He added and subtracted friends, employees, business associates, and others in the same way his bookkeeper added and subtracted digits. His motto was "In grain I trust." He protected his prosperity by building larger barns.

Jesus explained that the man had laid up his treasure for himself. He was the center of his own private universe, with his grain-god existing to provide for his needs alone. This man's values controlled him, but he didn't know it! He thought he was in control. In reality he was imprisoned within his treasure chest of values. They controlled what he did, what he thought about, and how he viewed others.

Can you think of ways your values about material possessions can imprison and control you? List several.

_____

_____

You may have noted ideas such as: *Often we get so accustomed to a certain standard of living that we feel locked in jobs that have ceased to be fulfilling. Or we may avoid certain friends because their lifestyle is more modest than ours.*

The rich man's values had isolated him. For example, he could not communicate with his god of grain. He could not experience prayer, worship, or fellowship with his grain. He could never receive guidance and direction, be affirmed, or be comforted by his god. Even worse, he was not free to give his grain away, for no god provided more. He had to hoard it! When he grew weak with age, there had to be more grain than he would have years.

A relationship with God shapes relationships with other human beings. When a person experiences no fellowship with God, relationships with others reflect self-centeredness, too.

A relationship with God shapes relationships with other human beings.

The more someone trusts in wealth, the less he trusts the motives of others. Each new acquaintance is suspect because the person may eventually try to tap the wealth. Having grain is neither moral nor immoral. The value placed on it is the important thing. Both the rich man, who mistrusted his poor relative, and the poor relative had the same value system. Both viewed wealth as a god.

With God, Christians experience prayer, worship, fellowship, guidance, affirmation, and comfort. Adam's children, persons apart from God, have no understanding of these intimacies. They have no day of worship, no prayer life, no expectation of guidance, no comfort. From the perspective of their value system, the things Christians spend their time doing are wastes of time. Adam's children cannot understand that Christians want to give their God to others. Persons apart from God are driven to protect their gods from others.

The man with the barns held a view that permits wealth to own persons, imprison them, twist every relationship out of shape. God said about him, "You fool!" The man forgot that his god of grain could not provide for eternity. In the end the god stored in the barns outlasted the man. When his soul was required of him, he discovered too late that his god was only stuff that would pass into the hands of another.

Another Scripture points out an additional problem when we value wealth. Read Matthew 6:19-21.

Jesus identified one of the greatest problems the children of Adam have to deal with: the erosion, decay, theft, and depreciation of the things they treasure. When the government taxes our treasures, we are allowed to depreciate their value each year. We can also deduct losses by theft. Billions of dollars are spent to protect or replace treasure. Insurance companies base their rates on the frequency thieves break in to steal. Security systems are big business.

The children of Adam have only one view of wealth, so they accept the inevitability of these problems. Too many Christians blindly accept this first view of wealth. Before you became a Christian, you collected your values related to wealth. Like the moths and the rust in the Scripture, those values are thieves. They steal from your intimacy with God and with others.

Unlike other values, the ones you hold involving wealth relate to your former gods. Before becoming a Christian, you trusted in something or someone. In what, or in whom, did you trust? What god did you select to provide for you?

Take this test. Recall the years when you lived without Christ in your life. Complete this statement: "In _____ I trusted." That is your "treasure upon earth." Have you been released from its power to rule over you? Does your former god still imprison you, hindering you from laying up true treasures in heaven?

In figure 15 the ball represents the god that ruled your life before you became a Christian. Each link in the chain is a former value related to wealth. Write in the illustration the god who controlled you and the values that bound you. After completing this exercise, take some time to ask God to free you from this "ball and chain."

Those who hold the first view of wealth ignore the future. Read 1 Thessalonians 5:2-6 and 2 Peter 3:7-13.

The people mentioned in 1 Thessalonians 5:2-6 go on storing up barns of grain, unaware of impending doom.

Review the following groups of verses. Then match each group with the statement that best expresses the concept in that group of verses.

____ 1. 1 Thessalonians 5:2-3
      2 Peter 3:7-10

____ 2. 1 Thessalonians 5:6
      2 Peter 3:11-13

a. God will not spare anyone in His righteous anger.

b. Christians should be alert and ready, expecting the Lord's return at any time.

c. The Lord is definitely going to judge the world at some point in the future.

You should have found that c was the best summary of 1 and that b was the best match for 2.

In view of the future, what value should be placed on wealth? The non-Christian answer to that began when philosophers concluded that life was meaningless. They did so by observing the emptiness within men who lived as prisoners of their own values related to wealth. They saw the world as uncertain and purposeless. Many of those philosophers actually committed suicide! Others decided that life should be spent enjoying sensations or pleasures. Above all, they taught that assuming responsibility for a purposeless world was absurd. Non-Christians who examined the first view of wealth became cynics.

Christians don't have to feel that way. They evaluate the first view of wealth through the teaching of Scripture. The day of the Lord will come as unexpectedly as a thief in the night and in a moment will sweep away all earthly treasures. Nothing we store up will endure.

Knowing this, should we accept the cynical attitude of the philosophers? Absolutely not! Second Peter 3:13 says, "We are looking for new heavens and a new earth, in which righteousness dwells." There is another comment about that Kingdom where there will be no moth, rust, or any other form of corruption or decay. God will bring a new heaven and a new earth into being. The beauty of this new creation will far surpass the beauty and splendor of anything our hands have ever created. Best of all, those who live in it will freely enjoy it all. Possessing nothing, they will enjoy everything!

Nothing we store up will endure.

INVESTMENTS THAT LAST

Yesterday you considered the first of two views of wealth. Recall what that view is and write it here.

The first view of wealth: _____

_____

The first view of wealth is that it is controlled by people and based on personal riches.

Read John 12:31 and 18:33-37.
In light of yesterday's study how should we live as Christians? The answer to that question is based on the fact that two kingdoms exist. One is the kingdom of this world. Jesus said that judgment rests on this kingdom and that its ruler will be cast out (John 12:31). Everything invested in that kingdom will become worthless. John 18:33-37 records part of a conversation between Jesus and Pilate. Pilate had no awareness of any kingdom beyond this world. Therefore, when he asked Jesus if He was a king, our Lord knew that Pilate referred to the kingdom of this world. Jesus said: " 'My kingdom is not of this world. ... My kingdom is not of this realm.' " Pilate did not

have the slightest idea what Jesus meant! Confused, Pilate asked: " 'So You are a king?' " Jesus stated that He was, and that His purpose for entering the first kingdom, the kingdom of this world, was to bear witness to the truth about the second Kingdom.

Pilate could not comprehend Jesus' words about the second Kingdom. He simply dispatched Jesus to be crucified and returned to his prison cell of values, where he lived a life of emptiness and tragedy. In Pilate's world people fought to get what they wanted. Jesus explained that His disciples were not fighting to keep Him from being delivered to the Jews. In other words, the second Kingdom has totally different values. People live by an entirely different set of principles. They do not invest their lives in that which is going to be consumed by fire. Instead, they invest in that which is transferable to the second Kingdom!

Many people today, like Pilate in Jesus' time, have no idea that two realms exist: the physical and the spiritual. They go through life immersed in the problems and preoccupations of this world, oblivious to their starving spirits. This total investment in the first kingdom is obvious in their lifestyles.

Decide whether each sentence describes a person investing his life in the physical world or in the spiritual world. Write *P* beside the statements referring to the physical and *S* beside those referring to the spiritual.

___ 1. Ed works an extra job mowing lawns on Sundays so that he can pay for his new videocassette recorder.

___ 2. Mary Ellen saves her lunch money every Monday to put in a special account for the mission group at church.

___ 3. Ruth stopped visiting elderly persons in a local nursing home because she works nearly 12 hours a day. She says her career is the most important thing in her life.

Did you write *P* beside 1 and 3 and *S* beside 2?

Read John 14:1-6.

Jesus declared that He would prepare dwelling places for us in the second Kingdom. With residences guaranteed, what should we take with us when we change addresses? What will last? Certainly not gold or silver, grain or barns. Is there anything that will transfer and not be lost?

The answer is in verse 6. Jesus explained that He is the way to the new Kingdom and that no one comes to the Father but through Him. The treasures that transfer are people! Only people will transfer from the first kingdom to the second Kingdom. Everything else will be destroyed.

Complete the following sentence.
Only _____ will _____

from one _____ to the next.

What, then, is the most important work for servants of God to engage in while living in the first kingdom? Since people are all that transfer from one kingdom to the next, we should prepare people to transfer to the new Kingdom.

And yet our possessions reflect what we value. As you look at your home; your investments; and, most of all, your use of time, ask yourself, *What will last when the fire comes?*

Another way to monitor your priorities is to take a look at your checkbook. It is a record in black and white of what you spend your money on and, therefore, of what you really value.

Examine your checkbook for the past two months. Then answer these questions. If someone didn't know you and had only your checkbook on which to base their opinion of you, what would they be likely to say about you?

_____

Are there any entries you might want to hide from your pastor? ❑ Yes ❑ No

Does your checkbook reflect mainly first-kingdom values or those of a citizen of God's kingdom? _____

If you answered first kingdom, what can you do to correct this?

_____

_____

The Bible reveals the values that will endure when our lives are over. Read 1 Corinthians 3:11-15.

Corporate officers anxiously study the quarterly profit-and-loss reports. The future of their jobs and the jobs of scores of

The treasures that transfer are people!

employees may well be determined by their companies' profits and losses. Adam's children take profit and loss seriously because in their value system, personal worth is determined by their ability to make a profit. Loss of wealth means loss of personhood. Adam's children also worship their treasures.

Carefully read 1 Corinthians 3:11; then answer the following questions.

What is Paul referring to when he says "foundation"?

_____

Who is the only true foundation?

_____

What other foundations do people sometimes try to build their lives on?

_____

Verses 13-15 give a hint about what eventually happens to people's foundations. What is it?

_____

You discovered that the foundation is the thing you value most in your life. You've built your life on it. Jesus Christ is the only true, totally secure foundation, although many people make wealth, success, or personal accomplishment their foundations. The Bible plainly says that everyone will be held accountable for his choice of foundation. They will be tested. Only those people whose lives are founded on Jesus Christ will pass the test.

How powerful is the issue of profit and loss in your treasure chest? What does a profit do to you? Are you continually dissatisfied with your salary? Do you react to a raise with a comment like: "It's about time! I'm worth a lot more than I am being paid"? Do you feel more valuable as a person when you receive a financial bonus? Does a future inheritance, to be yours when a relative dies, have more influence on you than you wish it did?

What does a loss do to you? For example, if you lost $10, how devastated would you be? Change the amount to $500. Now how bad do you feel? Your house is robbed, and your television and favorite pieces of jewelry are missing. Will you lose much sleep over it? You are on a bridge, and your camera falls into the river. How do you react and for how long afterward? Your lovely new car is sideswiped in a parking lot by a hit-and-run driver. What does it do to you?

Now is the time to reject the value system of the first kingdom. Refuse to use wealth as a means of feeling significant. Do not measure your worth by the amount of wealth you possess! Instead, measure it by spiritual wealth.

First Corinthians 3:11-15 tells us that we should be prepared for the fire's coming. If you spend your life investing in lumber, grain, and hay, the fire will leave you with nothing to show for your investment. Be wise enough, therefore, to invest now in a commodity that will transfer then. What can you take to the second Kingdom, the kingdom of God, that will pass safely through the fire? Only persons can be taken from the first kingdom to the second Kingdom! Persons are the "gold, silver, and precious stones," and "the fire itself will test the quality of each man's work."

What if the fire were to fall today? Would you carry any gold, silver, or precious stones to the new Kingdom? Who will go to the new land because you invested your life in them? Remember, what you value is who you are!

To sum up what you have learned about the first view of wealth, complete the conversation in figure 16 between a citizen of the Lord's kingdom and a citizen of this world.

> I believe that accumulating wealth is not as important as reaching persons for Christ.

Figure 16

Day 3

WHEN GOD CONTROLS WEALTH

You have considered the first view of wealth—the one most people have—that material possessions are the most important things in life. You learned, however, that this view ultimately leads to disappointment and wasted effort and time. Now we will examine the second view of wealth. As a Christian, you'll want to inspect carefully the values in your treasure chest about wealth and determine which ones need to be changed.

God owns it all! People own nothing.

Before you start today's lesson, fill in the thumb and forefinger in figure 17.

Did you write *One Source of Significance* on the thumb and *Two Views of Wealth* on the forefinger? Good! Now let's get started!

Why do sermons about money make so many people uncomfortable? The problem lies within their treasure chests! When ego and pride are tied to wealth, the personal control of it touches much more than money. A sermon on the subject becomes a threat to what makes people feel significant.

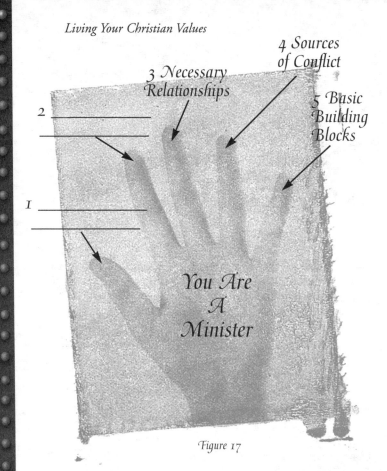

3 Necessary
Relationships

4 Sources
of Conflict

5 Basic
Building
Blocks

2 _____

1 _____

You Are
A
Minister

Figure 17

Paul settled who owns what with one short statement: "The earth is the Lord's, and all it contains" (1 Cor. 10:26). Those words eliminate forever the first view of wealth. God owns it all! People own nothing. Then the full impact of Paul's statement begins to be felt: if the Lord owns all the earth contains, then He owns the people in it, too. And the good news about that is this: if He owns you, He is obligated to care for you.

Philippians 4:19 belongs exclusively to the second view of wealth. Carefully read this verse. What does God promise to do?

_____

_____

If God is willing to supply all of our needs, then He will surely supply all of our wants as well.

❏ I believe this is true.
❏ I believe this is false.

What is the difference between a need and a want?

_____

_____

_____

How do we know which is which in our lives?

_____

_____

_____

After studying Philippians 4:19, you saw that God will supply all of your needs. But this verse doesn't mention wants, does it? So you should have checked the second statement. It may be difficult to explain the exact difference between a need and a want. But God knows the things that are necessary for your well-being. And that's part of trusting Him completely—you allow God to decide which is which!

This is a new theory about wealth, isn't it? If you came to Christ with your old values in place, you will have to rethink this subject.

Read Matthew 6:24-33, spoken by Christ, to understand this second theory of wealth.

Jesus said that everyone is a servant. The only question is, Which master do you serve, God or riches? The question cannot exist until you become a Christian and you have a choice of masters. Then the decision about which master to serve must be made and must be made deliberately. You are a Christian. Technically, you belong to God. But you will continue to feel a conflict inside you as long as you have not consciously and deliberately decided to be His servant in your day-to-day activities.

In figure 18, write your name and today's date. This will indicate your willingness to be God's servant and to make Him your Master. No more confusion about whom you're serving! If you really want to make this contract official, get witnesses to sign it, too!

CONTRACT

I, _____,
hereby proclaim that on the _____ day of
_____ in the year _____ I signed over control of my life to God through His Son, Jesus Christ. Furthermore, He is now rightfully my Master in all areas of my life, and I am His servant. I gratefully acknowledge that He, as my owner, will take care of me.

Your signature:_____

Witness:_____

Figure 18

If you commit your life to serving God, then He promises to care for you.

If you commit your life to serving God, then He promises to care for you. Yet those old fears of not having enough to survive haunt you. You were conditioned for years to believe that "the Lord helps those who help themselves." That is not in the Bible! You are to stop serving riches and serve God. Is it safe?

Saying that a person relies on God is not saying that a person has a right to be lazy or slothful or a right to expect others to provide for him the things he is able to provide for himself. Jesus said, " 'Do not be anxious' "—do not be concerned to the point of distraction. God will provide for you. Birds do not sow, or reap, or gather into barns. Yet since they are part of the world that belongs to the Lord, He feeds them. God is obligated as their owner to care for them. What about you? Will He do any less for you? Then there are the lilies. As lovely as they are, they " 'do not toil nor do they spin.' " Add grass to the lilies and it quickly turns brown and burns. Does God clothe lilies and grass? Yes, as their owner, He cares for them.

In Matthew 6:32 Jesus examines treasure chests to compare the value system of Adam's children with that of God's children. Your Heavenly Father knows exactly what you need. He will provide your needs. The second view of wealth gives you great freedom! What will you do with all the time you have since you have trusted your Owner with the responsibility of caring for you? Verse 33 gives the answer: " 'Seek first His kingdom and His righteousness.' "

A 50-year-old man said: "I long for the time when I will not have to struggle daily to make a living. One day I will have enough stored away to care for my needs, and I will retire. Then I will be able to enjoy life." Jesus is saying that you can retire right now from the first view of wealth! The Father owns you, and He is committed to take care of all your needs. Being freed from the first view of wealth frees you from bondage to your vocation. Whatever you do to provide the necessities of life for yourself and for others ceases to be a taskmaster that demands more and more of you. Your honest labor becomes a means of serving and honoring God.

Does it sound too good to be true? Well, it is true. It all begins when you throw out the old values in your treasure chest and live by the new ones. Make the transition! Say: "I am not my own master; I am owned by God. It is my responsibility to serve Him, and it is His responsibility to care for me."

Have you memorized this week's Scripture-memory verses? Write them in the next column.

Day 4

THE TREASURE WITHIN

Read 1 Corinthians 4:1-2 and 2 Corinthians 4:1-7.

These Scriptures describe the lifestyle of a Christian who has cleaned out the first view of wealth from the treasure chest and lives with the realization that the second Kingdom is coming. The servant's ministry has begun! Let's examine this person's lifestyle. This will give you a chance to see how similar your life is to the life of a servant of God.

Read each of the ideal characteristics of a fully-committed servant. Circle the number on the rating scale that represents where you are in your training for servanthood.

1. Servanthood has ended the search for significance (1 Cor. 4:1). This person is free to use every skill without a need to prove personal worth by doing so. The servant owns absolutely nothing; there are no personal possessions to protect. Being a child of God provides total significance and total freedom forever!

SECURE IN SIGNIFICANCE BECAUSE OF RELATIONSHIP WITH GOD

Very Secure				Very Insecure
1	2	3	4	5

2. The servant's assignment is to do the work of a steward (1 Cor. 4:1-2). The word steward describes a chief slave who supervises his master's household and property. He is entrusted with all of the master's assets. He gives proper rations at the proper time to all in the household. (That's why Jesus said we are to be "servant of all.")

SERVES OTHERS WILLINGLY AND JOYFULLY

Consistently		Occasionally		Rarely
1	2	3	4	5

3. No compromise is in this servant's heart (2 Cor. 4:1-2). Look at the list of old values that have been tossed out. This servant is totally committed to God.

COMMITTED TO SERVE GOD

Wholeheartedly		Mildly		Weakly
1	2	3	4	5

4. There is a special compassion for those who are "blind" (2 Cor. 4:3-6). Satan deliberately blinds the eyes of human minds to keep them from seeing the second Kingdom. Jesus said that His mission was to bring " 'sight to the blind' " (Luke 4:18). The One who is the Light of the world has "shone in our hearts" to bring light to blinded minds.

COMPASSIONATE AND INTERESTED IN NONBELIEVERS

Consistently		Occasionally		Rarely
1	2	3	4	5

Which area(s) do you need to improve in the most? Pick one area, pray about it, and make a conscious effort to dedicate it to God during the coming week.

One of the most beautiful and descriptive images in the Bible is the one Paul used in 2 Corinthians 4:7: "We have this treasure in earthen vessels." Ancient manuscripts were protected in clay jars, sealed at the top to keep moisture from eroding the documents. God's servant is pictured as being such an earthen vessel.

In the first view of wealth, riches glorify the body. People display their treasures by wearing them as adornments. The jewelry signals passersby that this human body contains a "very

God's servant is pictured as being such an earthen vessel.

important person." In the second view of wealth, riches are controlled by God. His servants display His wealth since they themselves own nothing. Their treasure, however, is not worn on necks and wrists. It is carried inside them, and it is of such great value that it cannot be compared to gold ornaments.

The plainly dressed body of a servant is not impressive; it is like a simple earthen vessel. But the love in the eyes, the gentleness of the touch, the warmth of the heart, and the compassion of the voice reveal a treasure contained within this life! There is a resiliency in the life of the steward who contains God's glory. Pressure, crisis, disappointment, the loss of all things touch the earthen vessel; love still flows. If the vessel is broken, the light of His glory contained within simply shines more brightly through the cracks.

Are you such a servant? Your Heavenly Father says to you: "My child, there is no need for you to spend your life striving to create a fortune. I own it all! Let Me provide for you. I'll advance you not only enough for your own needs but also enough to provide for others. Best of all, I will make you a

storehouse for the greatest of all treasures: I will place My glory within you! I ask only that you remain faithful to Me wherever you live and in whatever you do. My glory needs to be taken into factories, offices, schools, airplanes, mines, laboratories, and every other place in the world. With the other members of the body of Christ, take the treasure within your earthen vessel to all those places. This is My will for you!"

The Bible addresses these matters of serving others and sharing God's glory. Read Luke 16:19-26 and 1 John 3:16-18.

Like the self-centered man you met in day 1, this "certain rich man" believed he owned riches and had the right to spend all on himself. Completely oblivious to the needs of Lazarus, the rich man is a classic example of what was described earlier in 2 Corinthians 4:3-6. The "god of this world" had blinded his eyes with the hot poker of greed. He couldn't see a single way to use his wealth to help anyone but himself. He had been imprisoned by his value of wealth.

Think of an occasion when a brother's or a sister's need was obvious, but you or another Christian failed to notice and did nothing to help. Briefly describe such an incident.

_____

_____

Jesus said that when the rich man died, his imprisonment continued but without the comforts of home. Those who hold the first view of wealth live their lives in blind selfishness and their eternity in agony.

You, however, have an inheritance waiting for you in the life to come. Jesus has gone to prepare a place for you in His Father's mansion. That should be an exciting thought to you! Even better, you are not blind as the rich man was. There is an interesting parallel between John 3:16 and 1 John 3:16. John 3:16 states that God gave His only begotten Son, and 1 John 3:16 reminds us of our Lord's death. If Jesus laid down His life, we also ought to lay down ours for our brothers.

First John 3:17 explains that a true Christian cannot possibly go through life blinded to the needs of others. The eyes of God's children clearly see the Lazaruses around them. Theirs is the second view of wealth: they own nothing, God owns everything, and they are the stewards of His treasury. The Lazaruses of the world also belong to the Father, who loves them and cares for them. As the steward of the Lord's wealth, a Christian must stop and use it for a brother. That's the reason the steward has the world's goods!

Being a steward means learning to live simply so that others may simply live. It means becoming responsible for others, even if the others are irresponsible. The proof that God's love abides within is the way the world's goods are used. Many of us are so accustomed to an excessively high standard of living that we are not even aware of its extravagance. The Lord has blessed us with an abundance of this world's goods, but we tend to take our wealth for granted rather than to live simply, sharing with those who do not have enough.

For each area listed in figure 19, describe how you may have been extravagant at times. Then describe how you could live more simply in each area.

List several ways you could share your wealth with those who need help.

_____

_____

You may have mentioned sponsoring a child in a foreign country, contributing to a fund for relieving world hunger, adopting a child from a low-income group, donating clothes and furniture to a family whose home has been destroyed, or paying the tuition for a college student who can't afford it. These are only a few of many possible answers. The important thing is to put into practice your commitment to live simply.

Area	Too Extravagant	Simplified
Housing		
Vehicles		
Gifts		

Figure 19

Being a steward means learning to live simply so that others may simply live.

Decide now to simplify your life in at least one area and to share the excess with someone who needs it. Identify the area and describe how you can carry out your commitment.

_____

_____

Day 5

YOUR SOURCE OF SUPPLY

Those who are committed to the first view of wealth live defensively. Fear grips them when their riches are threatened. That's not true in the Christian's value system. God has given you His Holy Spirit. If He is willing to give you His own Spirit, do you think for a moment He would withhold lesser things from you? Life in the new value system is exciting! As His steward, you are responsible to provide His wealth to those who need it. Don't ever fear that if you give possessions away, they will not be replaced. You are at the end of a supply line that begins in His storehouse.

Do you need to go back to your treasure chest and throw out another of the values left over from your old way of viewing wealth? Do you fully trust your Lord to supply your needs? First John 3:22 reminds us that we are to depend strictly on the Lord for our needs: "Whatever we ask we receive from Him." If we truly believe this, then we need to replace fear of losing our possessions with faith that God will provide for us.

Read Luke 11:11-13; Mark 6:41-44 and 12:41-44.

Five thousand to feed with only five loaves of bread and two fish! Will God supply? If you ask Him for bread, what will He do? If you ask Him for a fish, what will He do? He will do a miracle! The mathematics of the second view of wealth are totally different from those of the first view. Jesus multiplied the loaves and fish by dividing them. As the disciples subtracted from the food by distributing it, He added to it until, at the finish, 12 full baskets were left over—1 for each disciple!

See if you can supply the answer to the equation below.

$$\frac{(5 \text{ loaves} + 2 \text{ fish}) \times \text{faith in God}}{5{,}000 \text{ men}} = \underline{\hspace{3cm}}$$

Your answer should be *12 baskets left over*. In the first view of wealth, people keep their eyes on the supply. In the second view of wealth, people keep their eyes on the Source. The fullness of God guarantees there will always be sufficiency. Learning to live by this value is stepping into a life of faith. Jesus watched the people at the temple treasury. Many rich people put in large sums. Then a widow dropped in two small copper coins. Jesus was deeply impressed! Calling His disciples, He said: " 'Truly I say to you, this poor widow put in more than all the contributors to the treasury; for they all put in out of their surplus, but she, out of her poverty, put in all she owned, all she had to live on.' " A widow, without any possible source of supply, gave all she had to live on!

Let's ask some different questions—ones that will probe into your treasure chest of values. Answer them honestly; God knows your true feelings anyway. If you discover that you need to make some changes, step out in faith and make them!

1. Would you give away something you needed in order to help someone else? ❏ Yes ❏ No
2. Are you willing to accept the reality that you don't own any of your possessions, that they belong to God? ❏ Yes ❏ No
3. If the Lord directed you to give away all of your possessions, would you do it? ❏ Yes ❏ No

These are hard questions, but they point to the fact that Christians must have different values in their treasure chests from the values of non-Christians.

A Christian received a request for a statement of net worth. After considering his assets and liabilities, he prayed: "Lord, I would like to report to You my liabilities. I am a sinner, with a heart that is deceitful and desperately wicked. I have repeatedly broken Your commandments. I have no righteousness at all. Next, I would like to report my assets. I have grace greater than all my sin. I have mercy, which has brought pardon for my transgressions of the law. I have the treasure of Your Holy Spirit dwelling in me. I have an inheritance waiting for me before Your throne. All this I have, and You provided it all. Now, Lord, I would like to report what You have entrusted to my care. You own a home titled to me on Your behalf. You own a car I drive. You own my family. You own my bank account. Master, I thank You for what I own, and I thank You for entrusting me with what You own. Amen."

Read 1 Kings 17:8-16 and Luke 4:25-26,28-30.

Living in the kingdom of God means that a whole new set of values begins to operate. No greater example can be found of how those values apply than the example recorded in the passage you just read. A famine had covered the land with death. Those with enough wealth to do so had migrated to other nations. Only the poorest of the poor had remained behind. One of them was a widow who lived in Zarephath with her son. They were at the end of life. Her child looked more and more like a living skeleton. Her own strength nearly gone, she forced herself to search for firewood to make one last fire, and then the end would come. God commanded Elijah to ask this starving woman for water and food. How odd of God!

Odd? Only if the scene is interpreted through the values in the first view of wealth. From that perspective each person must create the supply, and each person fears the loss of it. If she had

Christians must have different values in their treasure chests from the values of non-Christians.

been living by the old values, the widow might have refused to help Elijah.

Jesus told us that many widows around her might have taken such an attitude. All of them were living by the values of the first view of wealth. But God knew that this woman had a deep faith, and her value system needed affirmation. When she heard Elijah's words " 'Do not fear,' " faith exploded in her heart. Faith always walks by trusting the Father, not by examining reality.

What Elijah told the widow to do was utterly illogical based on the rules of the first view of wealth, but this woman believed in the living God. She did not live by the same rules as her widowed neighbors. She did exactly as she was told! Deep within her was the awareness that if she kept her eye on the Supplier rather than on the supply, all would be well.

The widow gave Elijah some of her water reserves and a bread cake before preparing for her son and herself. Her faith act began a miracle! In the same way Jesus added to the loaves that were being subtracted, God added to the barrel of flour and the jar of oil. Neither of them ever became empty. Her faith had triggered a supply always provided those who trust in God for their needs.

You may be wondering how this account applies to your life. Reread 1 Kings 17:8-16; then write three principles for dealing with wealth that this account illustrates.

1. _____

2. _____

3. _____

You may have found these three principles: *(1) Even though your natural inclination may be fear or anxiety, you should obey God when He commands you to step out in faith. (2) When you trust God for your needs, He will supply them. (3) Keep your eyes on the Source rather than on the supply.*

Jesus used this incident as an example in the passage you read in Luke. Why did Jesus select this widow's actions as an illustration of the faith walk? Jesus had read from the scroll of Isaiah in the Friday evening service in the synagogue of Nazareth. The Scripture witnessed that the Spirit of the Lord was on Him and that He would bring sight to the blind, freedom to the captives, good news to the poor, and so on. The most religious, synagogue-attending men in town said to Him: "Jesus, let's see You do that sort of thing. Go on. Show us that You have such power."

Although they were religious, their treasure chests were filled with the values of the first view of wealth. They knew all about selfishness, greed, fear, and pride. Jesus was very blunt with them. Using the illustration of the widow from Zarephath, He indicated that where faith does not exist, God's power is not seen. They were so angry that they tried to kill Him.

If you have never revised your values about wealth, you are not experiencing the supply God wishes to provide for you. What's more, if you don't decide to do something about it now, do you think you ever will? You cannot afford the luxury of living in the poverty of the first view of wealth. Step totally into the second view: God owns it all!

Let's review the concepts on the diagram of the hand and the two views of wealth. Fill in the blanks.

The thumb represents _____

The forefinger represents _____

The first view of wealth is _____

The second view of wealth is _____

Now here's your chance to show you've memorized your Scripture-memory verses this week. Write them here.

_____

_____

_____

_____

Did you do OK? If you had trouble with the verses, keep working on them. And by the way, when you go to church Sunday, don't forget what you've learned this week about being a steward of God's wealth. One of the best ways to share your abundance is to give to the ministries of your church!

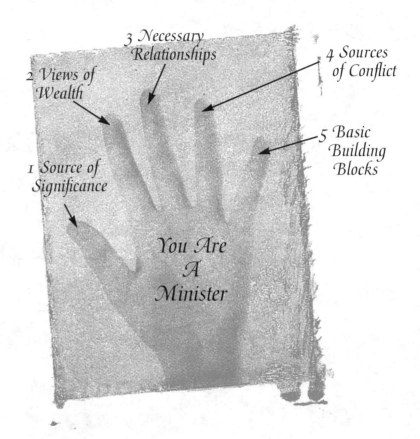

3 *Necessary Relationships*

4 *Sources of Conflict*

2 *Views of Wealth*

5 *Basic Building Blocks*

1 *Source of Significance*

You Are A Minister

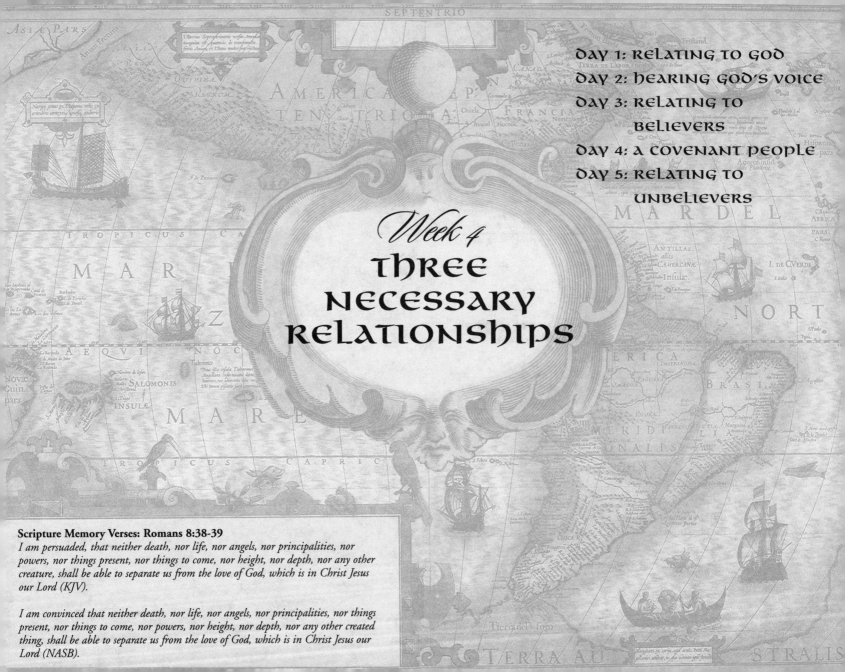

DAY 1: RELATING TO GOD

DAY 2: HEARING GOD'S VOICE

DAY 3: RELATING TO BELIEVERS

DAY 4: A COVENANT PEOPLE

DAY 5: RELATING TO UNBELIEVERS

Week 4

THREE NECESSARY RELATIONSHIPS

Scripture Memory Verses: Romans 8:38-39
I am persuaded, that neither death, nor life, nor angels, nor principalities, nor powers, nor things present, nor things to come, nor height, nor depth, nor any other creature, shall be able to separate us from the love of God, which is in Christ Jesus our Lord (KJV).

I am convinced that neither death, nor life, nor angels, nor principalities, nor things present, nor things to come, nor powers, nor height, nor depth, nor any other created thing, shall be able to separate us from the love of God, which is in Christ Jesus our Lord (NASB).

Day 1

RELATING TO GOD

Use your Scripture-memory card to begin memorizing Romans 8:38-39.

This week you will study three relationships you must have as a child of God and a true minister: God, believers, and unbelievers. First, let's review our diagram of the hand. In figure 20 fill in the thumb and the forefinger. Notice what is written on the middle finger.

Read Psalm 66.

The writer of Psalm 66 obviously had a vibrant relationship with God. He said, "Come and hear, all who fear [revere] God, and I will tell of what He has done for my soul" (v. 16). Recognizing that "He owns it all," he told the earth itself to shout joyfully and worship God. Like an excited child, he called, "Come and see the works of God … let us rejoice in Him!" (vv. 5-6).

There is a radical difference between the psalmist's worship experience and expressions of worship in many churches today in which participants focus on themselves or one another, completely unaware of God's presence. What is the difference? Fellowship. Many people may know about God, but they are not really with Him when they worship.

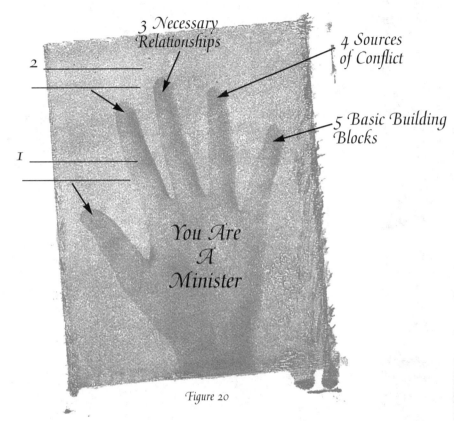

3 *Necessary Relationships*

4 *Sources of Conflict*

5 *Basic Building Blocks*

You Are A Minister

Figure 20

It's like that between many Christians and God. They know about Him by reading the biblical accounts of His activity, but they do not experience a deep relationship with Him. Look deep into your treasure chest and see if you can find a value inscribed, "Enjoy God forever!"

The psalmist valued his fellowship with God above all else. He revealed many facets of the relationship. It is obvious that he had spent a great deal of time with God. He had observed the way others paid Him lip service, giving only "feigned obedience." He had known God's protection and security because the Father watched over him. He had experienced God's discipline, for he had been "tried" and "refined … as silver is refined" (v. 10). His worship included sacrifices (v. 15). The finest animals were presented in appreciation and love. This man had had a long-term relationship with God; they had shared much, and they had shared over a long time.

You can describe your relationship with God just as the psalmist did. Each of the following verses describes a part of the relationship between God and the psalmist. Read each verse and then describe a specific incident from your life that illustrates this facet.

1. Read Psalm 66:5. Describe an awesome deed God performed in your life.

_____

_____

_____

2. Read Psalm 66:9. Describe a time God protected you.

_____

_____

_____

3. Read Psalm 66:10. Describe a hard time God used to improve your character or to strengthen you.

_____

_____

4. Read Psalm 66:13. Describe a sacrifice you made to show your love for God.

_____

_____

Read Hebrews 13:15-16.

Hebrews 13 offers suggestions about your fellowship with God. This passage suggests the sacrifices appropriate for you to offer God in your daily time of sharing. First is the sacrifice of praise, "the fruit of lips that give thanks to His name" (v. 15). Your prayer life is the means of offering this sacrifice.

Verse 16 lists sacrifices related to your ministry. Meditate on them: "doing good and sharing." These sacrifices involve, first of all, your time. Doing good means becoming a servant who cares and becomes involved in the lives of hurting people. Second, these sacrifices involve your stewardship. Sharing refers to your work as a steward. Possessing nothing of your own, you have been entrusted with His assets so that others may be cared for in His name. Your acts of ministry are acts of worship. God is more delighted by the sacrifices of doing good and sharing than He is with many formal worship services.

List the three suggestions the writer of Hebrews made for strengthening your relationship with God.

1. _____

2. _____

3. _____

Did you write praise God, do good, and share with others? Remember to put these acts of worship into practice every day!

The best part of having a vital relationship with your Lord and Master is what it does to your fears. Read Romans 8:35; 2 Corinthians 11:24-27; and Philippians 3:20-21.

List your three greatest fears.

1. _____

2. _____

3. _____

Always, in all circumstances, fear is the opposite of faith. The two words are as opposite as black and white. If you have fear, you do not have faith. If you have faith, fear is banished.

Paul showed fearlessness as he stated his faith in Romans 8:35. He listed some of life's greatest calamities. Nearly all of them are doubly dreaded because people feel helpless to protect themselves. Paul seemed to have no dread of those calamities.

In 2 Corinthians 11:24-27 Paul listed the calamities he had suffered during his ministry for Christ. Like Paul, you have the Holy Spirit to keep you in all situations, to be your strength, to be your friend in troubled times.

Have you ever considered the worst thing that could happen to you as a Christian? Would it be to die? According to Philippians 3:20-21, you already hold citizenship in heaven. Your body will be transformed to conform to the body of your Lord. If that's the worst thing that could happen to you, why are you afraid? It is much wiser to enjoy your new life in Christ, serving your Master without concern for what could go wrong.

In one of George MacDonald's novels, the hero spends three days alone with the New Testament to discover the secret of Christianity. The hero reports that it boils down to three propositions:
1. It is a person's business to do God's will.
2. It is God's business to take care of that person.
3. Therefore, a person should never be afraid of anything.
You see, being a servant obligates the Master to care for you in every situation. Fear is an absolute contradiction of faith!

George Mueller set out to show the world that God can meet every need. By faith he built many orphan houses in which several thousand children were housed and fed. His policy was to keep the needs of the orphanages a closely held secret. He reasoned that he was doing the work God had called him to do as His servant; if he faithfully did the work, then God would supply all of the needs. If those needs were revealed, his dependence on God would end. On one occasion a wealthy

You have the Holy Spirit to keep you in all situations, to be your strength, to be your friend in troubled times.

woman asked: "How much do you have in the bank?" Even though only a few pennies remained in the treasury, Mueller replied: "Madam, we have a bank that cannot be broken [bankrupted]!"

Year after year no one knew the status of the orphanages until the annual report was released. Shock waves passed through England again and again when the depth of Mueller's faith was revealed. Accounts would dip to practically nothing, but never did they go into the red. To Mueller it was very simple: if he did God's work, the Master would supply.

Look at your three greatest fears you recorded earlier. Write three reasons you don't have to be afraid of these anymore.

1. _____

_____

2. _____

_____

3. _____

_____

Take a moment to reflect on your fears and to evaluate your faith. Both are values. Only one can be in your treasure chest. Which one occupies it at this moment? If you are relating to your Master, you will never be afraid of anything!

ҺEARING GOD'S VOICE

When you entered God's kingdom, you became a servant to God and people. As His servant, there is something you need before you are able to serve Him. You see, servants do not decide what's best in life. Masters do that. When the Master decides what's best, then His servants do what's best. You can't act until you have learned God's will, and you can't know His will before going to the Listening Room. What is the Listening Room? It is the place where God speaks, outlining His will for His servant. After you have heard His plan, you can pray with authority, for you are asking according to His will. Asking for something before you know His will is presumptuous!

Knowing God's will is extremely important. As His servant, you genuinely want to please Him; but sometimes, when faced with a choice, you're not exactly sure which path to take. Are there areas in your life in which you must make a crucial decision, but you're not sure what God wants you to do? Read the list on the following page. Check each area that applies to your life; then write beside it the specific problem you're having in knowing God's will in that area.

❏ Family: _____

❏ Vocation: _____

❏ School: _____

❏ Church: _____

❏ Relationship: _____

❏ Finance: _____

❏ Other (specify): _____

Today you will discover ways to discern God's will.

Read 1 Samuel 3:1-10.

Samuel, a young follower of God, did not yet know about the Listening Room. Verse 7 explains, "Now Samuel did not yet know the Lord, nor had the word of the Lord yet been revealed to him." The word for *know* is an important one. It refers to intimacy, a thorough knowledge of another person. Samuel had not matured in his relationship with God; as a result, he did not know when God was speaking and when He was not speaking.

Is that your problem? If it is, take heart from the principle set forth in this account: if you are not sure you are hearing God's voice, keep listening! God patiently called Samuel four times before the lad realized what was taking place. Until you know what God's voice sounds like, proceed slowly.

Notice the second thing that helped Samuel. He got the counsel of a more mature person who knew what it was to hear God's voice. God would probably not lead another person to tell you directly what God's will for your life is, but God does work in clear patterns among all people. Those who have been on the journey before you can help you in your beginning steps.

Listen for a word about what God is doing, not just for what you will do.

Write the first two suggestions for learning God's will.

1. _____

2. _____

Did you write in the blanks *keep listening* and *get counsel?*

First Samuel 3:11 outlines how God began to reveal to Samuel what He planned to do about Israel and about Eli. Note that God told Samuel what He would do, not what Samuel was to do! The Master does not relax while the servant works; instead, the servant assists the working Master.

This is one of the important facts about what you hear in the Listening Room! Listen for a word about what God is doing, not just for what you will do. If you get the big picture, God will give you specific instructions from time to time as you serve Him. To relate to your Master effectively, learn to listen. The Listening Room is not an optional value for your treasure chest; it's the compass that guides you in your journey.

Read Psalm 1.

Perhaps you would like to ask this question: "Should I expect God to speak to me in an audible voice?" Nothing in Scripture rules out that possibility if He chooses to do so. However, it is unlikely that you will ever hear God speaking to you that way. The reason? God speaks in a far more powerful way than directly to your ear! This "voice" is described in Psalm 1. In verse 1 the writer rejects all counsel from the wicked, the sinning, and the scoffers. Then in verse 2 he goes to the Listening Room. There the "voice" speaks God's plans to him: he "hears" the law. The word law refers to the teachings of Jehovah God. In past centuries His words were carefully recorded for others to study. The One who inspired the writers to record them is the same Holy Spirit who lives in you! Studying or reading the Bible is an important way to know His will.

The psalmist said that he delighted in the teachings of Jehovah God; he spent countless hours in the Listening Room, meditating day and night on them. The Bible should be your constant companion. You will often hear the Bible called the Word of God. He speaks to all persons through it. In fact, this written Word is so important that you may be absolutely certain about this: no person ever receives another word from God that is not in harmony with the Bible. Many cults claim to have received a later word from God. This "later word" often contradicts the Scripture. These groups are not of God.

Read Joshua 1:8.

This verse also refers to the importance of the law as a way to hear God speak. Once again it calls for day-and-night meditation on it. Every value in your Christian walk is to be found in its pages, along with counsel about every problem.

Carefully look again at Psalm 1:2-3 and Joshua 1:8. What is the result of meditating "day and night" on God's Word?

_____

Did you see that the result is success? Check the statement that seems to explain best the biblical idea of success.

❏ 1. To have many material possessions and much wealth.
❏ 2. To live confidently and overcome problems effectively.
❏ 3. To be popular and well thought of.

Did you check *2?* God's promise of success refers to success in doing His will. What more could we ask for than a guarantee that everything God asks us to do, we will be able to do?

Long after Jesus had ascended into heaven, James confirmed that nothing has changed in the way God speaks to persons in the Listening Room. Read James 1:25.

James encouraged Christians to look "intently at the perfect law." God's Holy Spirit had continued the work of inspiring men to write down God's words, updating the law to include the record of Jesus' coming, the beginning of the early church, and the instructions for living as servant-ministers of Christ.

Psalm 1:1, Joshua 1:8, and James 1:25 also emphasize another requirement for knowing God's will. Read these verses again. Did you notice the words *does not walk, stand, sit, do, abides by it,* and *effectual doer?* All of these words refer to actions. It is not enough to look at and hear God's Word to know His will and be successful. You also have to do His will!

A central theme of Jesus' teachings was that a ritual practice of religion can never substitute for a life of righteousness or for serving and ministering to others. Things have not changed much after two millenniums. The greatest enemy of the gospel is church-sponsored activity that becomes an end in itself while an untouched world suffers.

Satan neutralizes Christians by offering good tasks that stop them from doing the right tasks. In Jesus' day the Pharisees ignored hurting people in their world and occupied themselves with such "clean" activities as tithing, praying five times a day, fasting, making proselytes, and studying Scripture. Who can fault such respectable activity? Jesus did!

Read the following situation and choose the best response:

You are getting ready to walk out the door on the way to your midweek Bible study. The phone rings. It is Rebecca, your next-door neighbor. She's sick and needs you to keep her daughter for her while she goes to the doctor. You—
❏ 1. stay home and keep her daughter;
❏ 2. tell her you're busy and go on to your Bible study.

Hopefully, you chose *1*. Romans 2:13 makes a terse statement about how we hear God's voice in our Listening Rooms: "Not the hearers of the Law are just before God, but the doers of the Law will be justified." The purpose of God's written Word is to equip the minister for service. The doing of the law is the proof that it has been heard.

How do we hear the law? We link hearing the law with doing the law. Where will we hear His voice? Where the law is being practiced! Servanthood is learned not in the club room but on the practice field. The Pharisees taught in the temple; Jesus taught in the fields. The Pharisees avoided the unclean; Jesus was known as the friend of winebibbers and sinners. The Pharisees left the wounded bleeding on the road; Jesus healed those who had need. Where will you find Jesus, God's Son, the Servant of people? You will find Him where the law is being practiced.

Do you understand now how this concept of hearing God's voice works? To test yourself, pretend that you're talking to a friend who has just become a Christian. He asks you, "How do I know what God wants me to do?" What would you tell him? Write your answer in figure 21.

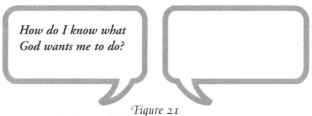

How do I know what God wants me to do?

Figure 21

Did you include such things as *listening to God, getting counsel from wise Christian friends, meditating on the Bible,* and *doing (practicing) what you hear God say?*

Read James 1:21-27.

James repeated what Romans teaches: "Prove yourselves doers of the word, and not merely hearers who delude themselves" (Jas. 1:22). Again, in verse 25, he stressed: "One who looks intently at the perfect law, the law of liberty, and abides by it,

The purpose of God's written Word is to equip the minister for service. The doing of the law is the proof that it has been heard.

not having become a forgetful hearer but an effectual doer, this man shall be blessed in what he does." In verse 27 James was specific about the meaning of being "doers of the law": "This is pure and undefiled religion in the sight of our God and Father, to visit orphans and widows in their distress, and to keep oneself unstained by the world."

Ministry to orphans and widows is not the only ministry God expects. What are specific ministries you can perform today or this week in the name of Jesus?

_____

_____

_____

_____

Remember, in practicing God's Word, we hear God's voice!

The ministry God has called you to is not just to distribute information about Jesus Christ; it is to wash feet, heal the brokenhearted, and weep with those filled with grief. If you wish to hear God's voice speaking to you, go to the right location. He waits for you beside a neglected child, a hungry family, an alcoholic, or a self-righteous neighbor. He is speaking to you. Can you hear Him? He is saying something like: " 'To the extent that you did it to one of these brothers of Mine, even the least of them, you did it to Me' " (Matt. 25:40).

RELATING TO BELIEVERS

"I am so disillusioned!" the young Christian said to the pastor. "When I came into the church, I thought I would find almost perfect people. Instead, I found regular, everyday people."

You barely enter the household of faith before seeing that Christians are far from perfect. The Bible never promised that Christians would be perfect until after they receive glorified bodies in the life to come. As long as we live this life, we will experience maturity mingled with immaturity. Christians can live in victory over sin and should. However, as long as we are human, we will never achieve sinless perfection. Nevertheless, the second vital relationship in your Christian life is with fellow believers. There are no "Lone Rangers" in God's kingdom. You need the members of the body of Christ, and they need you. God uses your relationship with other Christians to shape and refine your life. In turn, you are His instrument to bless and shape their lives.

In your treasure chest, value the body of Christ. You may not spend eternity with all of those in your human family, but you will spend it with those in God's family. They are there to serve you, and you are there to serve them. It is true that you are the church in the world and that you are on mission to serve those who are not yet in Christ. However, being the servant of all begins with your fellow church members. Learning to love and serve them is vital to your Christian life.

For example, consider the servant ministry Romans 12:6-16 calls for. Read that passage.

Realize that each assignment relates you to real people, all imperfect, all on the journey with you, and all in your church! Review Romans 12:9-16. In these eight verses find and list at least 10 different suggestions of ways you can serve your brothers and sisters in Christ.

1. _____   6. _____

2. _____   7. _____

3. _____   8. _____

4. _____   9. _____

5. _____   10. _____

You could have listed any of the following: *love without hypocrisy, be devoted to one another, avoid evil and seek good, give preference to one another, serve the Lord enthusiastically, rejoice in hope, persevere in tribulation, devote yourself to prayer, give financial assistance to needy Christians, be hospitable, be kind to those who are unkind to you, be happy with those who are happy, grieve with those who are grieving, treat everyone the same, don't think you're spiritually wiser than everybody else.*

Now let's get specific. After each of the following questions, write the name of a person in your life to whom it applies.

To whom should you give preference? _____

Whom are you lagging behind, perhaps slowing them in their journey toward Christian maturity by not being fervent enough in spirit as you serve the Lord?

_____

Who needs to rejoice in the hope you could bring to lift their discouraged spirit?

_____

Who needs your example of how to persevere in tribulation?

_____

Who can share your devotion to prayer? _____

Which saint needs your financial assistance? _____

Who awaits your hospitality? _____

What neurotic Christian is attacking you, needing your blessing in response to jealous words?

_____

In your treasure chest, value the body of Christ.

With whom should you rejoice, and with whom should you weep?

_____

This is the ministry you have to your brothers and sisters in God's family: to meet each need with the gifts He has entrusted to you and to be shaped in turn by theirs.

What special talents or gifts do you have that you could use to serve the needs of your brothers and sisters in Christ? (Paul suggested several in Romans 12:6-8, if you need help getting started on your own.) List at least three specific gifts in figure 22.

1. _____

2. _____

3. _____

Figure 22

Read 1 Thessalonians 4:9-12.

What gifts do some of your Christian friends have that you benefit from? Or to put it another way, What do you need from your Christian friends? Name three needs and, if possible, name the Christian brother(s) or sister(s) who can help fulfill those needs.

1. _____

2. _____

3. _____

In 1 Thessalonians 4:9-12 God's family is admonished to "love one another." That love is to be characterized by a lifestyle described in verse 11. In your own words write a summary of that lifestyle.

_____

_____

Steadiness, faithfulness, and dependability bring harmony to the "one-another life." The reason for that lifestyle, said Paul, is "so that you may behave properly toward outsiders and not be in any need." The term outsiders refers to unbelievers. The church never sees itself living in isolation; its ministry is to outsiders. In this day of endless stress and pain, Christ's body is to be a place of steady peace and love. What a haven for hurting outsiders!

Do you begin to see the church in a special way? View the family of God loving one another, patiently caring for one another. Then, and only then, will you see the renewal of an almost extinct form of evangelism. This form of evangelism does not happen through sermons and visits by the pastor. The evangel is not one person acting alone. Rather, the evangel is the collective body of Christ. The church's "one-another" life witnesses to outsiders. Its testimony is not just what it says but the way it lives. The most powerful form of evangelism available today is the lifestyle of the transformed community of God. Will you resolve to be a powerful force in that witness?

Have you learned this week's Scripture-memory verses? Write them here from memory.

_____

_____

_____

_____

_____

Day 4

A COVENANT PEOPLE

They sat in a circle, candles burning. A slave sat beside his owner. A rich man removed his cloak and put it over the shoulders of a shivering woman. A girl sat quietly beside her uncle, remembering the jeers her parents threw at them as they departed for this gathering. Two students sat with their tutor.

Quartus spoke: "We know that the edict of Nero has forbidden us to meet together. Let us pray that our Lord will return soon, establish His reign, and release us from this situation." Several said, "Amen!"

Quartus guided the group to share the Supper of the Lord. He described the final supper of Jesus with His disciples. He left out none of the particulars, as shared with him by James in Jerusalem. "Finally," said Quartus, "Jesus said that this act between us would be a new covenant, sealed in His blood. We recognize that our life together is the life of a body and that Christ is its head. Our commitment to Him involves an equal commitment to one another. We are the body of Christ, and He is our head."

The most powerful form of evangelism available today is the lifestyle of the transformed community of God.

In unison they repeated: "We are the body of Christ, and He is our head." Quartus continued: "You have judged the body rightly. He has not only given us Himself but has also made us His body. We are one in Him." Again they repeated, "We are one in Him!"

A loaf was broken, distributed to all, and eaten in unison. The cup was passed from lip to lip. The experience was so powerful, it almost seemed that a new light had entered the room. "We shall finish as Jesus did with His disciples: after they sang a hymn, they went out. Let us leave one by one, quietly. Speak not to one another until you are far away from here."

In the middle of the quietly sung psalm, the door was smashed open by two powerful guards. Twenty soldiers forced the members of the circle into the street outside. The captain of the guard laughed harshly and said: "Just the right group to entertain Nero! Take them to the arena!" In less than an hour the group found themselves holding one another in the center of the arena, packed with thousands of screaming people. They could barely see Nero as he brought down his hand, signaling the release of lions nearly insane with starvation. Later, Nero walked to the middle of the arena, his way lighted by a torch. After studying the mutilated, dead bodies, he said in exasperation: "These Christ-worshippers! To the last moment they sought to care for one another. Look how they held one another's dismembered bodies as they died. What causes them to stick together? There is something about their religion I do not understand!"

Do you understand it? How would you characterize the atmosphere in the church you are now a part of? Is it warm? Is it friendly? Is it like the group you just read about, or is it more like a secular social club? Describe it.

_____

_____

_____

The Lord's Supper is shared by the body of Christ, not by just anybody. The bread and the cup remind us not only of Christ's death but also of our life—the "one-another life."

Read 1 Corinthians 11:23-29 and fill in the following blanks with the missing word or words.

In the Lord's Supper the bread represents Jesus' _____

given as a sacrifice for our sins. The _____ represents

His blood, which is the new _____. When we

eat and drink, we're remembering _____

_____ until He comes again.

Your answers should be: *body, cup, covenant, Jesus' death.*

In your treasure chest, value your relationships with your brothers and sisters. Through the centuries others have had to pay a price you may never have to pay for your life together. Then again, you might. Never forget that!

Not all Christians were as close as the ones described in today's material. Read 1 Corinthians 11:17-22,27-34.

Acts 8:1-4 records that the Roman persecution separated the Christians in Jerusalem and sent them in small groups to live in other parts of the empire. Little did Rome know how God would use that action to spread the gospel. Everywhere the Christians went, the Christian witness sprang up because of the way the Christians shared the gospel.

Well … nearly everywhere! The group who went to Corinth did not do so well. After their relocation they had a treasure-chest problem! Jewish values did not fare so well in the lust capital of the empire. Located on a little strip of land between two major bodies of water, their new town was filled with pagan and immoral influences.

Conflict between Christian values and Corinthian values began to take its toll. One man had an affair with his father's wife. Critical spirits, fed by guilty consciences, fractured the life of the little group in the church. Spiritual gifts were used as toys for play and for private, personal enjoyment. Embarrassed by their lack of fellowship with the Master, Christians found little basis for fellowship with one another. A selfish spirit replaced their servant spirit. Gatherings were marked by strife. Factions and divisions devastated their meetings.

First Corinthians 11:17-21 describes some of the problems the Corinthian Christians were having. At the top of the next column, match the Scripture on the left with the description of the problem on the right by placing the letter beside the appropriate number.

___ 1. Verse 17

___ 2. Verse 18

___ 3. Verse 19

___ 4. Verse 21

a. The church was divided.
b. The Corinthians were not sharing their food at the fellowship suppers.
c. The church's fellowship suppers were actually adding to the problem rather than helping it.
d. Factions existed.

The answers: *1. c, 2. a, 3. d, 4. b.*

The Christians at Corinth were still going through the motions of worship, but the reality of being the body of Christ had vanished. They were similar to clouds with no water. When servanthood is lost, the body of Christ is dead. What replaces it is an ugly and self-serving assembly. When they tried to share the Lord's Supper, there was no intimacy, no love. The feast time was marked by self-serving actions. No common meal was shared; each family brought food and ate separately from the others. As a result, one drank too much wine while a poor family ate little or nothing.

How different from the church they left behind in Jerusalem! There they had gone from house to house, breaking bread and sharing their wealth as needs arose. Here they had kept the form of a body of Christ, but the life of that body was dead.

Think about your own church for a moment. What was the most recent Lord's Supper like? Was it a truly worshipful experience or an empty ritual? Describe at the top of the next page your feelings about it.

When servanthood is lost, the body of Christ is dead.

69

_____

_____

_____

Paul bluntly told the church to "judge the body rightly" (1 Cor. 11:27-29). The Lord's Supper is, in addition to the remembrance of Christ's sacrificial death, a renewal of a contract among the people who compose His body! Therefore, to eat the bread and drink the cup without having a proper relationship to those in the family is unworthy—and the person who does so eats and drinks judgment to himself.

How important is it for you to value highly the body of Christ? Paul seemed to think it important enough that those who abused their relationship with the body of Christ stood in danger of severe chastisement from God (1 Cor. 11:30). In our day many Christian organizations plead for financial support and call for believers to participate in their projects. Many of these causes may be commendable, but not a single one can replace the ministry of the body of Christ, where people live in covenant relationship with one another. Indeed, if the body of Christ were functioning properly, not one of them would even be needed.

Of course, the other side of the coin is of equal concern: many groups call themselves a church but lack a covenant relationship among the members. Commitment to a church structure can be vastly different from a commitment to one another in Jesus Christ! The church in Corinth did not live. It was half dead when Paul wrote to it, and within a century it had decayed into oblivion. Not long after that, John wrote to seven churches (Rev. 1—3), of which only two had real life remaining. Today some churches are alive; others are dying; some are dead. When a dead church comes to life again, we say that it has experienced a revival. Precious indeed are those who can be used by the Spirit to bring a revival to the body of Christ. Be someone who can be used this way.

Read the following statements and, on the basis of what you've learned today, decide whether each is true or false. Write *T* beside true statements and *F* beside false statements.

___ 1. The Lord's Supper should be taken seriously and participated in reverently.

___ 2. There's no need to examine your relationship with Christ and His body before participating in the Lord's Supper.

___ 3. Improper observance of the Lord's Supper is the only unforgivable sin.

___ 4. The Lord's Supper is a time to renew the contract among the people who compose the body of Christ.

___ 5. The Lord's Supper is not a time to remember the sacrificial death of Jesus.

The answers are: *1. T, 2. F, 3. F, 4. T, 5. F.* How did you do?

RELATING TO UNBELIEVERS

Read Romans 1:16 and 9:1-5.

The first necessary relationship in your life is with your Master. The second one is with the body of Christ. The third one is a special relationship with the children of Adam—those who have not yet become Christians. They need to be adopted, and Paul said it is their right to be (Rom. 9:4). The Father wants every person everywhere to be adopted into His family, and He has provided for every person a place in His household of love (Rom. 1:16). Your Master's primary work is to adopt all of the children of Adam who will agree to be adopted.

Read 1 Timothy 2:1-4. What does verse 4 say is God's attitude toward unbelievers?

_____

God wants all people to come to know Him in a personal way, and He expects you to be by His side, working with Him to bring people into His family. Being among unbelievers is not always enjoyable, is it? Their habits, language, treasure chests of values all conflict with your own. Yet your presence among those who do not know Christ is at the very heart of your work as a minister. Seeing a person's potential to become a child of God is the way you bring hope to that person.

Read Romans 10:1-4. What did Paul say in verse 2 about the Jews' feeling toward religion?

_____

_____

Paul said that the Jews had "a zeal for God" but that it was a mistaken zeal. Read verse 3 and summarize what it says.

_____

_____

The Jews were very religious, but their religion was based on their own achievement of righteousness rather than on faith in God. In a sense they were wasting their time being religious, because they were operating with the faulty assumption that they could earn a relationship with God by being good. Many nonbelievers today also think they can earn salvation by being good.

Name places you normally go in the course of your day where you're likely to be associated with nonbelievers.

_____

_____

Your presence among those who do not know Christ is at the very heart of your work as a minister.

For each place you named, give an example of one way you could minister in that situation. Be specific.

_____

_____

_____

Read John 4:35-36.

If you ever feel that you would like to withdraw from ministry and simply enjoy fellowshipping with other believers, stop and think! Who would go to the white (ripe) fields Christ spoke of? Who would do the harvesting? Do not think that church staff and missionaries should go on your behalf to the harvest. Can you imagine a group of 30 laborers applauding the owner of the farm as he harvests 100 acres of wheat alone?

Consider the great pain Paul felt as he wrote the verses you have read today. His love for the people of his own race was intense! He knew the emptiness and wretchedness of their lives, because he had experienced that emptiness and wretchedness himself. Paul recalled his life when it was separate from Christ; he compared it with the unbridled joy he had come to experience. He described how terribly it hurt him that they were not yet adopted as God's children. Paul said that he would be willing to forfeit heaven and spend eternity in hell if it would mean their salvation (Rom. 9:1-5).

It would be valuable to you in the years to come if you would write a description of what your life was like before Christ entered it. Record the memories of emptiness, futility, fear, pride, desire for immorality, and other feelings that marked your lifestyle. Then if you ever find your concern for the unreached growing dim, reread that description and let it renew the fires of compassion in your heart! Take a few minutes to make your diary entry in figure 23.

Dear Diary,
Before I became a Christian, my life was …

Figure 23

If you ever discover that you are so busy in the church that you do not have time to relate to unreached persons, you are too busy. Remember, you are on mission to white fields. Jesus continually associated with the children of Adam, loving, healing, caring, forgiving. His special relationship with them proves that you must have one, too. If God's Son could live on this earth and not become bottled up in religious activity, you have no excuse for doing so. You need a special relationship with the children of Adam. They need to be adopted!

How many persons do you associate with on a regular basis? How many of them are unbelievers? Ask yourself, If I do not share Christ with these friends, who will? God has placed you in a small world of your own; in that world you are His missionary. If you fail to minister in your world, you have no right to expect someone to come into your world from the outside to minister to it. It is you, or it is no one. Make a commitment now to be aware of opportunities to witness in your world.

John, a leader in his church, carpooled with three others each weekday to the office. The group discussed every imaginable topic. However, John, feeling that religion was a private matter, avoided the subject. After a year had passed, one carpooler suddenly died without having become a Christian. Does John stand accountable to God for the man's destiny?

Romans 10:12-15 explains that two factors are involved in every unbeliever's conversion. Read these verses; then answer the following questions. Verse 14 names the first factor in the conversion process. What is it?

_____

The first factor is *hearing the good news*. But how are unbelievers to hear the good news, according to verses 14-15?

_____

The news must be *spoken*. And that's where you come in. Unless you carry out your responsibility to tell the good news to the people in your world, someone may never hear it. You are accountable for this—which leads us to the second factor. Read verse 13 to discover it. What is it?

_____

The second factor in the conversion experience is *responding*.

You have no responsibility for how persons respond when they hear the good news. But you are responsible to see that they hear. You are God's voice to those in your world. If you remain silent, they will not hear. For that you are accountable!

Read Ezekiel 3:18-19. Answer the following questions.

Which verse relates to the first factor of conversion mentioned in the previous paragraphs? _____

What is that factor? _____

Which verse deals primarily with the second factor? _____

What is that factor? _____

For which factor will you be held accountable? _____

You are God's voice to those in your world. If you remain silent, they will not hear.

The longer some people live as Christians, the more isolated they become from unbelievers. If you have no unbelievers in your life, you do have unbelievers related to the persons in your life. Can you think of anyone related to someone in your life who isn't a Christian with whom you could share Christ? Write the name.

_____

If you don't know anyone, make a conscious effort to find out about the people related to your family and friends. Someone's eternal destiny may depend on your effort and concern!

Let's review important concepts you've studied so far.

How many necessary relationships are there? _____

Name them.

1. _____

2. _____

3. _____

How many views of wealth are there? _____

Name them.

1. _____

2. _____

How many sources of significance are there? _____

Describe it.

_____

_____

Write your Scripture-memory verses for this week.

_____

_____

_____

_____

_____

Close this week's study in prayer. Pray specifically for your relationships with God, believers, and unbelievers.

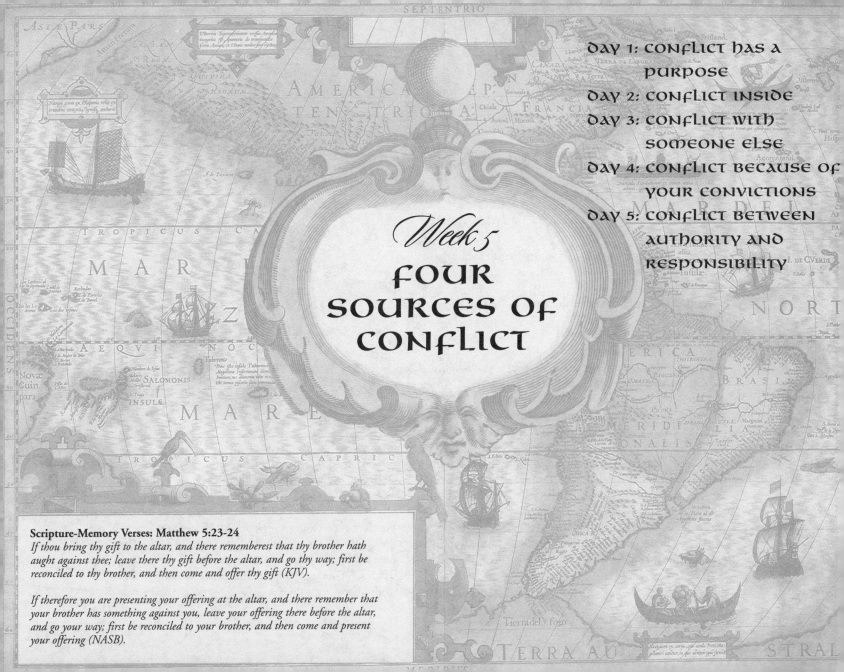

DAY 1: CONFLICT HAS A PURPOSE

DAY 2: CONFLICT INSIDE

DAY 3: CONFLICT WITH SOMEONE ELSE

DAY 4: CONFLICT BECAUSE OF YOUR CONVICTIONS

DAY 5: CONFLICT BETWEEN AUTHORITY AND RESPONSIBILITY

Week 5

FOUR SOURCES OF CONFLICT

Scripture-Memory Verses: Matthew 5:23-24

If thou bring thy gift to the altar, and there rememberest that thy brother hath aught against thee; leave there thy gift before the altar, and go thy way; first be reconciled to thy brother, and then come and offer thy gift (KJV).

If therefore you are presenting your offering at the altar, and there remember that your brother has something against you, leave your offering there before the altar, and go your way; first be reconciled to your brother, and then come and present your offering (NASB).

Day 1

CONFLICT HAS A PURPOSE

Use your Scripture-memory card to begin memorizing Matthew 5:23-24.

Write the missing phrases on the hand in figure 24.

Did you remember: One Source of Significance, Two Views of Wealth, and Three Necessary Relationships?
Have you ever felt downright stupid because you handled a conflict the wrong way? Welcome to the human race! Would you like some help cleaning out your treasure chest, pitching out some old—and stupid—ways of handling conflict and putting some new—and right—ones in their place?

This week we will look at four sources of conflict: (1) conflict inside yourself, (2) conflict with someone else, (3) conflict because of your convictions, (4) conflict between authority and responsibility.

Which of these four sources of conflict do you feel gives you the most trouble in your life? Write it here.

_____

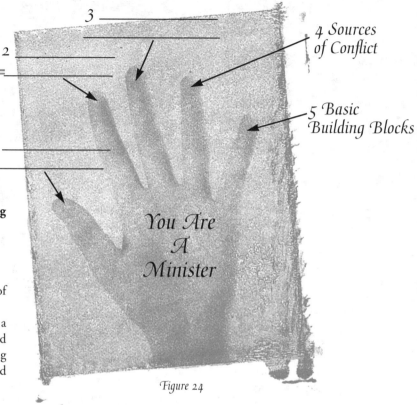

3 _____

2 _____

1 _____

4 Sources of Conflict

5 Basic Building Blocks

You Are A Minister

Figure 24

As you study, be especially aware of any suggestions that will help you overcome the conflicts caused by this particular source.

Westerners preparing to live in the Orient are warned about the importance of "face" among Asians. To lose face is to undergo shame or loss of dignity. To save face is to keep your self respect or good reputation. It's serious business, and it works both ways. When you keep face, not even a slight embarrassment is permitted. Practically all of your old values for handling conflict relate to saving face—namely, yours!

How significant is saving face to you?

_____

To what degree are you willing to manipulate your life and others' lives to avoid your embarrassment or humiliation?

_____

_____

Have you ever been guilty of lying or covering up the truth to protect your reputation? Explain.

_____

_____

How does remembering this incident make you feel now?

_____

_____

Before you became a Christian, your significance was the most important thing in life. To keep that significance, competitiveness became a part of your nature. Society says: "Win at all costs! Measure significance by winning! Hate losing and hate losers!" If losing an argument, a tennis game, or the profit

from a business deal causes you to feel that you have lost face, you still have false values about status in your treasure chest. Sometimes you are tired, sometimes you are sick, and sometimes you must work in an area beyond your expertise. When those times come, you may be tempted to measure yourself by old standards and consider yourself insignificant. Nonsense!

Take a lesson from Paul. Read Philippians 1:12-24.

Paul was the most "celebrated" missionary of his day. Notoriety and status were not among his values. It was important, however, to some Christians in Rome. Perhaps they were jealous of Paul's travels or of the number of churches who read his epistles. Whatever the motive, they watched with pleasure as he endured house arrest, planning to proclaim Christ themselves and gain the laurels. Paul saw right through them! He explained that they "proclaim Christ out of selfish ambition, rather than from pure motives, thinking to cause me distress in my imprisonment" (Phil. 1:17). Conflict was caused by a desire to be significant!

When you face conflict, ask yourself, Do I have to win this battle in order to save face? If the answer is yes, have a quick prayer meeting about your sin of pride. You see, the trouble with living sacrifices is that they keep crawling off the altar!

Write one verse from Philippians 1:12-24 that summarizes how you should feel about your relationship to this life's goals and ambitions and how you should feel about Christ.

_____

_____

When you face conflict, ask yourself, Do I have to win this battle in order to save face?

Now restate the verse in your own words.

_____

_____

Did you identify verse 21? This verse says that Christ is the main focus of your life; therefore, nothing in this world can hold you, bind you, or cause you any ultimate loss. Acknowledging this fact can free you from the constant conflict of trying to protect your ego from bumps and bruises!

Moreover, conflict has an important purpose for a believer. Read Hebrews 12:3-15.

"Lord, why must conflict exist at all? As a Christian, I expected peace in my life. Conflict because of unresolved values within my own life, conflict with another person, conflict because of my convictions, conflict between authority and responsibility—four sources of it! Could you not just erase them all?" Yes, God could have done exactly that—but He did not. Instead, He chose the Calvary road, the thorns, the cross, even for His own Son. Hebrews 12:3 explains that Jesus received the torture inflicted by hostility and conflict "so that you may not grow weary and lose heart." He has walked in your shoes. Furthermore, He has walked where you have never walked, as verse 4 states. The next time you feel like throwing a pity party, consider Hebrews 12:5-7.

Write at the top of the next column a one-sentence summary of Hebrews 12:5-7. Refer to this summary to keep in perspective conflict in your life.

_____

_____

You'll have your own summary, of course, but one possible summary is: The Lord's discipline is a proof of His love for me. You must learn to handle conflict properly if you are going to mature as a Christian. Let God use each conflict as a means of sandpapering the rough edges off your character. Verse 11 says, "All discipline for the moment seems not to be joyful, but sorrowful; yet to those who have been trained by it, afterwards it yields the peaceful fruit of righteousness." God knows areas of spiritual growth are needed in your life that require your struggling with various kinds of conflict. Not one conflict in your life is unimportant! Each is part of His prescribed treatment for you.

Does this view of conflict help you accept it better? Think of a situation in your past that was troublesome at the time but that God used to teach you important lessons. Complete the following facts about that situation.

Nature of the conflict: _____

Duration of the conflict: _____

Solution of the conflict: _____

Result: _____

Area of spiritual growth: _____

Identify from Hebrews 12:10 God's objective for your growth.

_____

_____

God's ultimate objective is for you to share His holiness. The result of conflict, properly handled, will be "straight paths for your feet," the healing of limbs, peace with all people, and especially "the sanctification without which no one will see the Lord." That word *sanctification*, you may recall, means to be made holy. Learning to deal properly with the four types of conflict you will study this week will develop holiness.

Verse 15 gives a careful caution when walking through the minefields of conflict: "See to it that no one comes short of the grace of God; that no root of bitterness springing up causes trouble, and by it many be defiled." God's grace, "unmerited favor," permits us to avoid what we deserve from the Father. We are to extend such grace to those who do not merit it. Above all, a Christian is to beware of roots of bitterness springing up. Bitterness is one of the most powerful weeds to grow in a human heart. If it is not snipped as it springs up, it will grow so rapidly that it will overtake the entire life.

Understanding the purpose for conflict will make it possible for you to pray before it, pray through it, and thank God after it that He used the conflict to shape your Christian character. Above all, remember that He does not send anything to you that will destroy you. His desire is to mature you!

CONFLICT INSIDE

Inner conflict can be described as a war between values, fought inside your treasure chest. Those from your former years and those from your new life in Christ have been permitted to coexist. The condition requires your immediate attention!

Read Luke 22:54-62.

This passage records the terrible inner conflict Peter had to struggle with at the time of Christ's arrest and trial. Peter loved Christ and was devoted to Him, and he was committed to the things Christ had taught him during the past three years. That love and commitment kept Peter near Christ even in the midst of false accusations, mockery, and denial. But Peter also had another value—his own personal safety. When people began to identify Peter with Christ, Peter began to fear that he might suffer the same fate Christ was suffering. Crash! The two values clashed head-on.

Read again Luke 22:61-62.

Can you imagine the embarrassment, the self-accusation, the sense of utter failure, and the abject desolation Peter must have felt in that moment? But that is not the end of the story.

Inner conflict can be described as a war between values, fought inside your treasure chest.

Read John 21:15-22.

Notice how Christ later used Peter's traumatic experience as a backdrop to help him resolve his inner conflicts and choose the values he would keep.

No one likes to be embarrassed in front of others or to be crushed with a sense of failure. But sometimes such experiences can be enlightening. As He did with Peter, Christ can use your bad experiences for your good—if you will let Him.

Can you think of a time in the past when you failed or were embarrassed, but through that experience you learned something valuable? Describe that experience, highlighting the lesson you learned.

_____

_____

James 4:8 provides the formula: "Draw near to God and He will draw near to you. Cleanse your hands, you sinners; and purify your hearts, you double-minded." When inner conflict appears, seek God and His will for you. Confront the double-minded values that make your treasure chest a battleground.

How can you put this verse into practice? List practical steps you can take to "draw near to God."

_____

_____

You may have listed things like: *Spend time in confession and prayer, asking God to forgive my double-mindedness. Read and study the Bible, looking for God's will for me. Be open to God's presence in everyday events and relationships.*

Philippians 3:13-14 recommends that you decide there is "one thing I do"! Read those verses. The heart that is set to serve God without tolerating old values knows peace. The remainder of those two verses describes a life without inner conflict, a life that puts away old values and commits only to the new ones. Summarize those verses.

_____

_____

Philippians 3:13-14 is a wonderful motto for life! Describe the visual image you see with your mind's eye when you read it.

_____

_____

You may see something else, but one strong image is of a runner who is about halfway through a race. She may be getting tired; but instead of slacking off, she forgets the miles she has already run and concentrates on her goal—the end of the race. Remembering your goal is an excellent way to streamline your Christian walk and to reduce conflict in your life.

Entering servanthood requires a radical change in life patterns, leaving no room for old values that say, "I want to play master!" Happiness is the result of a choice you make in life. When you choose to serve God as your only Master, it's amazing how simple life becomes. In Philippians 4:11 Paul revealed the complete lack of conflict within himself by declaring: "Not that I speak from want; for I have learned to be content in whatever circumstances I am."

Can you make that statement? If not, what values are waging within your treasure chest? Read the following list and circle the values that are causing conflict with your most important value, serving Christ.

unkindness	materialism
impatience	gossip
greed	lust
pride	selfish ambition
faultfinding	prejudice
indifference	dishonesty
fear	anger

A solution to these conflicts was given earlier in the lesson. Write it here.

_____

Did you write *draw near to God* and *purify your hearts* (Jas. 4:8)? When proper values are placed in the treasure chest and old ones are tossed out, Christians possess peace in the midst of discord.

Let's consider a biblical example of internal conflict. Read Acts 10:1-16.

From Peter's first contact with Christ, old and new values continually collided within him. His thirst for significance and his hunger for truth conflicted again and again.

Examine the following list of characteristics that describe Peter. Some are admirable traits, and some are not. Read each verse; then match it with the character trait it best exemplifies.

_____ 1. Matthew 26:69-74	a. impulsive
_____ 2. Acts 3:1-7	b. cowardly
_____ 3. Acts 10:25-26	c. courageous
_____ 4. John 13:8-9	d. dishonest
_____ 5. Mark 14:70-71	e. compassionate
_____ 6. Acts 4:17-20	f. humble

Your answers should be: 1. b, 2. e, 3. f, 4. a, 5. d, 6. c.

Peter lost a battle the night Jesus was arrested, but he won his war with Satan! With abandon and zeal he later faced the same religious leaders who had arranged his Lord's death and fearlessly accused them of murdering God's Son. Facing prison did not trigger compromise in him; he would never deny Christ a second time.

Peter began his ministry for Christ as a servant-priest, working exclusively among the Jews. Being a Jew himself, Peter felt quite at home with the customs, the language, and the religion. What about Gentiles? The possibility of taking Christ's

When you choose to serve God as your only Master, it's amazing how simple life becomes.

message to them had not entered his mind. The reason was in his treasure chest! Peter was totally unaware of a value he had picked up while probably still a child. It was a solid, brick-wall prejudice that excluded Gentiles from his life.

Peter was not alone in his attitude. The newly organized church in Jerusalem was exclusively Jewish, and the disciples at this point saw nothing wrong with that. Jews thought exclusively of themselves. Do you? Do you feel deep concern for those who starve in northeastern Africa or for the unreached Muslims of Afghanistan? When you pray, how wide a circle of people do you cover?

On a short holiday in Joppa, Peter had a vision in which he saw a large sheet coming down from the sky. All sorts of "non-Jewish" animals were there! God's voice spoke to Peter: "Get up, Peter. You are hungry; go kill, and eat the flesh of the animals." An old value inside Peter rebelled. "Peter," the value said, "you are a Jew, and Jews don't eat any of those animals." Peter said aloud: "No, Lord, no!"

How ridiculous! You can say *no* or you can say *Lord*, but you cannot say no to your Lord. The two words cannot coexist. Peter's prejudice and his Lord were in conflict. The battle raged, according to Acts 10:16, through three skirmishes before Peter rejected his old value and accepted a new one.

Figure 25 will help you sort through your treasure chest and identify values you may need to eliminate. Have you ever had an experience in which you felt the Lord wanted you to do something that was against your value system, and you tried to say to Him, "No, Lord, no"? Write below **some of the values you had to get rid of in order to do God's will.**

Values I have to eliminate to do God's will:

_____

_____

_____

_____

_____

Figure 25

When the new value came into Peter's life, he was able to become a servant-priest to all people. The result was the conversion of the Gentile Cornelius. Who knows? Maybe your Lord will give you a vision for going to the very persons you have never considered important enough to associate with, the people who need God's forgiveness and love as much as you.

Write your Scripture-memory verses for this week.

_____

_____

CONFLICT WITH SOMEONE ELSE

Nothing is more miserable than an unsolvable conflict with another person.

Have you ever been involved in a conflict with a fellow Christian that seemed unsolvable? ❏ Yes ❏ No **If yes, describe the nature of the problem.**

_____

_____

How did you settle it? Or did you?

_____

_____

If you solved it, are you satisfied with the way things turned out, or do hurt feelings remain?

_____

If you are still in conflict with that person, read on to find out how you can resolve the conflict. If you have already resolved the conflict, compare the process you followed to the process you will study today.

In Philippians 4:2 Paul said that Euodia and Syntyche should "be of the same mind in the Lord" (KJV). Once again we are introduced to double-mindedness, this time between persons. The problem of God-given values conflicting with self-serving values is now causing a new type of problem. Was the source of the conflict within Euodia's treasure chest, Syntyche's, or both? The text does not say. However, any one of the three possibilities might be correct.

In verse 3 Paul called on the whole church to help mend the breach between them. When two within Christ's body conflict, they must settle it between themselves or seek counsel from the body. Scripture outlines the procedure for doing so.

Step 1 is in Matthew 5:23-24. Describe that step.

_____

_____

Did you write something like _seek reconciliation with the person with whom I am having a conflict?_ Take the initiative to seek reconciliation with the other person. Whatever the cost, it is worth it to be at peace. Don't worry about saving face! Make the first move, no matter whose mistake created the conflict.

Nothing is more miserable than an unsolvable conflict with another person.

Step 2 is in Matthew 18:16. What is that step?

_____

_____

If the two in conflict cannot settle it between themselves, they then agree to get counsel from a mutual friend or friends within the body. Often others see us more clearly than we see ourselves. The objectivity of such counsel will be a maturing experience for both persons. Although painful, this sandpapering of their lives will produce sensitivity and maturity in them both.

Step 3 is in Matthew 18:17. Describe that step.

_____

_____

A conflict between two members disrupts the church's harmony and must be settled. The matter is to be brought before the body. A public meeting to minister to two persons in dispute is touchy! Such a congregational meeting should take place in an atmosphere of prayer, love, and tenderness.

Step 4 is in Matthew 18:17. Describe this step.

_____

_____

The stubborn person is not to be abandoned by the church but rather is to be treated " 'as a Gentile and a tax-gatherer.' " On one hand, this final step accepts the reality that this person is in rebellion. On the other hand, this step acknowledges the church's continuing responsibility to serve that individual with the same spirit of compassion exhibited toward an unbeliever. The relationship is not severed, only revised.

Matthew 18:21-22 answers a question that will help resolve many conflicts. What is that question (Hint: Peter asked it), and what was Jesus' answer?

The question: _____

The answer: _____

How will this guideline help you handle future conflicts with fellow believers?

_____

_____

The question is: *How often do I have to forgive someone who has wronged me?* The answer is: *As many times as necessary!* This guideline should make you aware of the need for a forgiving spirit. Many times conflicts that could normally be solved quickly are turned into major, ongoing feuds because one or both of the persons refuse to forgive.

Should Christians go to court against each other? First Corinthians 6:1-8 is so precise and so binding that there can be no question about the answer. Read those verses. Under no circumstances are Christians to go to secular courts to settle any dispute between themselves!

Conflict with someone else is painful. What should Christians do when they cannot see eye to eye and cannot settle their conflict easily?

Paul and Barnabas faced such a situation. Read Acts 15:35-40 and 2 Timothy 4:11.

The two missionaries served side by side to establish many churches in the Roman provinces. They took along young John Mark, Barnabas's nephew from Jerusalem, as an apprentice. They first traveled to the island of Cyprus, then to Pamphylia on the mainland, where John Mark left to return home. Later, Paul and Barnabas returned to Antioch. After months of ministry they had become close friends, and they understood each other well. Paul was intense, strong-willed, totally committed to the task. Barnabas, whose name means "Son of Encouragement," was gentle, sensitive, a peacemaker.

When time came to return to the work, Barnabas insisted that John Mark be given a second chance. Paul thought John Mark had showed himself to be unreliable and did not want to take him. The Greek word for sharp disagreement in Acts 15:39 is the mother of the English word paroxysm and describes a passionate conflict between the two. Paul and Barnabas could not reconcile their difference, and neither could yield to the other.

Then they found a solution. They would separate, making possible both desires. Barnabas would go to work accompanied by John Mark, and Paul would take Silas with him. When Paul and Barnabas had settled the issue, the church was able to commit them to the grace of the Lord, and they departed. Nothing in Scripture suggests that they departed as enemies. Their mutual ministry ended, but their respect for each other did not die. It's obvious that both Paul and Barnabas were sincere in their beliefs. Their disagreement wasn't an ego struggle. It was genuinely a matter of differing commitments.

Mutual respect eventually brings healing.

Later, John Mark was again involved in Paul's ministry (2 Tim. 4:11). Permanent, ugly prejudice was not a part of the apostle's character. With greater maturity John Mark was gladly welcomed to Paul's team.

What did these two missionaries teach us by the way they handled their passionate conflict?

1. Christians do not reject one another. Differences of viewpoint may be permitted, but banishing someone from your life is unacceptable. Christians aren't perfect—just forgiven!
2. Christians do not always agree. It is unrealistic to think that they will. Sometimes both parties hold justifiable positions.
3. Sometimes the best solution is to allow two positions to coexist. Demanding instant compromises to disagreements may lead to broken relationships, which cannot be easily mended. Had Paul and Barnabas been filled with ego, each would have fought to conquer the other. They might have embroiled the entire church in their dispute, bringing pain to many innocent people. Fortunately, each was mature enough to realize that going to the mission field together was not mandatory; respecting each other in Christ was!

4. Time and space are important factors in solving conflicts. They allow healing and may lead to later closeness.
5. Mutual respect eventually brings healing. This is what the Father wants. Blessed are those who come to the end of a conflict by praying together!

Construct a step-by-step solution to the following case study of a disagreement between two Christians.

Lynn and Jan colead a youth discipleship group in their church. Having worked together for five years, they enjoy a close friendship and respect each other's leadership abilities. Recently, however, they've run into a conflict. Lynn believes that only youth who have been active and committed to the youth group throughout the school year should be allowed to participate in the summer mission trip. Jan believes that any youth who want to go should be able to, provided they attend pretrip training sessions. This conflict threatens to disrupt the plans for the trip. How can these two sincere Christians solve their problem? Try to incorporate the five principles you learned today.

_____

_____

_____

_____

_____

Day 4

CONFLICT BECAUSE OF YOUR CONVICTIONS

The corruption in the church of Martin Luther's day revolted him. He wrote 95 statements about needed reforms, all supported by Scripture. When his theses came to his superiors' attention, he faced an order to recant all of the 95 accusations. He stood before the tribunal and declared: "I cannot recant! Here I stand! God help me!" God did help him, and history was affected by one man who stood for his convictions.

In Luther's treasure chest was a single value that prepared him to face death rather than compromise what he knew to be true. Christians throughout the centuries have readily surrendered their lives rather than their beliefs. Do you possess that value?

Read Acts 4:1-20.

The Council in Jerusalem imprisoned Peter and John for proclaiming Christ. In Acts 4:17 they decided " 'in order that [the gospel] may not spread any further among the people, let us warn them to speak no more to any man in this name.' "

If you knew, as did Peter and John, that the death penalty might be the result of sharing your faith, what would you do? Perhaps the question is too distant from the world you live in to be answered fairly. Let's look at some more appropriate questions. What would you do in these situations?

On a business trip your group is going "out on the town," which means partying, drunkenness, and possibly sexual immorality. You know that your boss will either fire you or demote you for not participating. How would you react?

_____

_____

_____

You attend a party. Pot and cocaine are brought out, and a lot of pressure is put on you not to be a "party pooper." How would you handle the situation?

_____

_____

_____

By concealing some funds, you can get a huge tax deduction. It's not exactly wrong, but it is open to question. Does it have to be illegal to be morally and ethically wrong? Is your Christian responsibility to the law only, or does it include ethical considerations as well?

_____

_____

You bump into another car in a parking lot. Your car is not damaged, and no one saw you. Is getting caught the only reason to confess you have damaged someone's property?

_____

_____

_____

You need a supply of pens at home. A box of them taken from work would never be missed. Where do you draw the line between what you deserve from your employer and what he deserves from you?

_____

_____

_____

You are visiting a town. You could visit an X-rated theater, and no one would know. Do you think that what you do when you are alone is no one's business but your own? Or does your status as a servant of God require total purity?

_____

_____

_____

When your boss goes out of town, you know that you can get away with not doing your job. What would you do?

_____

_____

_____

Christians throughout the centuries have readily surrendered their lives rather than their beliefs.

Which of these situations causes you the most difficulty in taking a stand? Explain.

_____

_____

This may be an area in which you need to reevaluate your convictions. Any conviction you would be willing to compromise is not a true value! If you are not fully aware at all times of the values you are committed to, life can be treacherous for you.

You will not travel far in your Christian journey before you will be stunned by the sordid activity of someone you respect as a "mature" believer. That person will permit certain beliefs, accepted only some of the time. Learn from his actions the importance of clarifying your values. It could happen to you!

Paul's comments in 1 Corinthians 9:24-27 reveal that we never reach a time in life when we can say: "I have arrived. I'm faultless. I'll relax!" Read the verses, and then write *T* beside true statements and *F* beside false statements.

_____ 1. It's OK to be halfhearted about your Christian commitment because only one person wins anyway.

_____ 2. Self-control is a necessary trait in a Christian.

_____ 3. You should have definite goals in your Christian life.

_____ 4. The goal you'll achieve as a committed Christian is only temporary.

The answers should be: *1. F, 2. T, 3. T, 4. F.*

Conflict over convictions is not a problem when there are well-defined values in your treasure chest that are as important as breathing itself. When you are your values and your values are you, to betray them is a form of self-destruction!

What values are ultimate in your treasure chest? In figure 26 write several values you consider more important than anything else in your life.

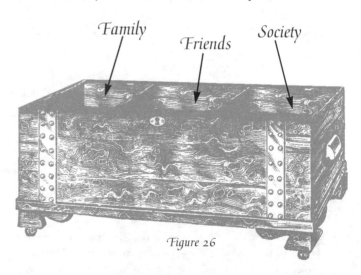

My Treasure Chest of Values

Family   *Friends*   *Society*

Figure 26

An ultimate situation was faced by Nate Saint, Jim Elliot, Pete Fleming, Roger Youderian, and Ed McCully. These young missionaries believed that evangelizing the murderous Auca Indian tribe was more important than their own lives. The five set up camp on the Curaray River, deep in the heart of Ecuador's jungles. Holding notebooks filled with Auca phrases, the men smilingly greeted the first naked men who approached their tree hut.

Four of their bodies, found by the search party, were pierced with spears. The butchered body of Ed McCully had been swept away by the currents of the Curaray, to be eaten by piranha. Their commitment to their values had caused them to die.

Not all Christians value their convictions above their lives. Like Peter, they choose to deny their Lord rather than risk their lives. After Peter faced his ultimate situation and denied his Lord, his value in that area was forever changed. Even so, he still possessed a desire to be approved by others.

Read Galatians 2:6-14.

Peter's conflict related to associating with Gentiles. God had shown him in Joppa that salvation was for both Jews and Gentiles. Nevertheless, the "pillars" of the Jerusalem church had strong prejudice against associating with Gentiles, and Peter feared their criticism. As long as the others from Jerusalem were not around, he freely ate with the Gentiles. Then, when the leaders who seemed to be important arrived, Peter immediately withdrew from eating with the Gentiles. His double-mindedness infuriated Paul! In front of the Jerusalem group Paul rebuked Peter, exposing his former conduct before the very people Peter wanted to please.

Peter's double-mindedness provides us an important lesson: conduct that varies to please people or suit conditions reveals double-mindedness! You need to choose values consistent with God's teaching and stick to them, regardless of the cost.

If you are a value and a value is you, it will never be adjusted to surroundings! Your ultimate values will bring you into conflict with your surroundings and with other persons, but you will never have an inner struggle over the position you should take. On the other hand, if you have an inner struggle over what you should do and if it is possible for you to adjust your behavior to suit the circumstances, the values in that area of your life are not ultimate values.

Can you identify one or two areas in your life in which you tend to allow other people and outward surroundings to dictate your behavior? Read the list of life areas and check the areas in which you need to strengthen your values.

❑ Telling the truth
❑ Treatment of people who are different from me
❑ Behavior in social situations
❑ Honesty in business dealings
❑ Sexual purity
❑ Commitment to church activities
❑ Behavior at work
❑ Other: _____
❑ Other: _____
❑ Other: _____

You need to choose values that are consistent with God's teaching and stick to them, regardless of the cost.

How can your hypocrisy and lack of consistency hurt other people? Give an example to support your statement.

Did your answer include the idea that people trust you to behave a certain way in certain situations? They put confidence in your dependability. When you vacillate and change, they don't know whether to trust you. This can hurt your family and friends, as well as non-Christians who may be watching your life carefully.

Checking out the values in your treasure chest is a nonstop assignment. Throw out those that do not glorify Christ and commit to those that are ultimate values for you. Decide now that you will not waver when it is time to take a stand for Christ.

CONFLICT BETWEEN AUTHORITY AND RESPONSIBILITY

God did not create us to be masters but to be servants. The central fact about servanthood is that there is a Master who decides what's best. Children are unfortunate when Mom's decision can be negotiated and changed by complaining to Dad and when Dad's strictness can be canceled by manipulating Mom. A marriage is wretched when a husband and a wife constantly fight each other for the right to be in control. There is a great turnover of employees even in Christian organizations when the lines of authority and responsibility are not clear. God's principles apply equally to all situations.

The lines of authority were not clear in the early church, and no one acted responsibly. Read 1 Corinthians 14 to see what was happening. Paul's solution to the problem is recorded in 1 Corinthians 14:40. Write that solution here.

Some of the people at Corinth were rebellious and were leading others to reject the authority of Paul's teaching. Paul wrote 2 Corinthians 10—13 to insist on his responsibility to speak about conditions in the church and to defend his authority to do so. Are you unhappy because of a conflict between authority and responsibility? Perhaps you have a tendency to be rebellious against authority, or perhaps you find it impossible to exercise control over an area for which you are responsible. Either way, Ephesians 5:21-33 states God's values that belong in your treasure chest.

Read Ephesians 5:21-33; then match each Scripture verse on the left with its summary on the right.

_____ 1. Verse 21

_____ 2. Verse 22

_____ 3. Verse 25

_____ 4. Verse 28

_____ 5. Verse 30

a. A wife should respect her husband's responsibility to lead and to provide for the family.

b. There should be mutual respect in a Christian marriage.

c. A husband should love his wife as much as he does himself.

d. All Christians are members of Christ's body.

e. A husband should love his wife as Christ loved the church—sacrificially.

I hope you got these answers: *1. b, 2. a, 3. e, 4. c, 5. d.*

Ephesians 5:21-33 states God's values that belong in your treasure chest.

The first point, in verse 21, is that we are to "be subject to one another in the fear [reverence] of Christ." Mutual respect among the various members of the body of Christ is to be a living example to the watching world. Next, the mutual respect between a husband and a wife is used to illustrate the principle. The wife is to respect her husband, and the husband is to love his wife. Don't misinterpret this passage to be a put-down of women. Notice that the husband is to love his wife as Christ loved and gave Himself for the church. This passage does not teach that a husband controls his wife as though she is an object. True love for each other causes each person to give and receive responsibility and authority in the relationship.

First John 5:16-18 deals with another area of potential conflict involving responsibility and authority: a situation in which two are equals and neither has authority over the other. Read those verses. What should you do when you see a fellow Christian doing a wrong act that will hinder his spiritual growth and will blemish the church's witness?

_____

_____

_____

You should pray for that person. But is praying all that should be done? No!

Read 1 Thessalonians 5:14-15.

What should be done for the unruly? (*Unruly* means soldiers who are out of step or who have broken ranks.)

_____

_____

What should be done for the feebleminded (discouraged and disheartened)?

_____

_____

What should be done for those whose faith is weak and incomplete?

_____

_____

Fellow Christians need to be warned, exhorted, encouraged, supported, helped, and guided. They need positive, redemptive actions carried out in a spirit of patience and from a desire to do good for the person. Galatians 6:1 warns you not to try to deal with such a person unless you are spiritually mature enough to do so with a genuine spirit of meekness and a sincere desire to restore fellowship with that person and redeem his witness.

When a person's authority is not recognized, a person cannot assume responsibility in that area. Chaos results, with conflict and frustration reigning. Rebellion against authority causes misery to all involved!

Read Genesis 13.

Lot had been invited to join Abram in his journey to the place God had set apart for him. Abram was the elder, the leader, the patriarch, the most venerated of all the family members. In the sight of both God and people Abram was the leader of the clan. Nevertheless, Lot had a selfish, independent spirit. When they arrived at Bethel, Lot refused to honor his uncle's rightful position of authority. His rebellion against authority soon spread to all of his herdsmen. Soon the clan was divided between those who were loyal to Abram and those who were loyal to Lot. For Abram the place of God's appointment had become anything but paradise. In the presence of the pagan Canaanites and Perizzites, two men who both claimed personal commitment to Jehovah were having a problem! The name of their Lord was being disgraced by Lot's insubordination. What should Abram do?

The situation could have continued endlessly if Abram had not acted. The way Abram handled the situation was the right way. God commended him for his decision! Abram reasoned:

1. I cannot be responsible for one who refuses to accept my authority.
2. Discipline, therefore, is impossible.
3. The insubordinate person will not seek to solve the problem; I must take the initiative.
4. The way I handle the problem must reveal my personal faith in God.

5. My action must require the insubordinate person to face personal responsibility for every action.

Have you ever been involved in a conflict when you were the one in authority? ❏ **Yes** ❏ **No If yes, describe the nature of the conflict; then apply the five-step solution in day 3 to resolve the conflict. If you haven't been in a conflict like this, use one in someone else's life.**

_____

_____

Abram followed this pattern. He did not try to discipline Lot. (1) He decided how to deal with the problem. (2) He witnessed to the Canaanites and Perizzites of his own faith; they would know that his trust was in God. (3) He generously permitted Lot to choose any part of the territory he desired. (4) In the future Lot would have to accept personal responsibility for his own life.

What Lot chose for himself, as expected, was the choicest portion of the land. What he had also chosen for himself, he would discover, was the ultimate loss of all his possessions, his wife, his daughters, and his personal integrity. Abram's principles brought him God's blessings, land beyond his wildest dreams, and the promise of descendants who would become as numerous as the dust of the earth. Those principles are often painful to apply, but they always bring peace to end conflict.

Viewing those principles from the viewpoint of the subordinate person's position is also significant:

1. I am responsible to the person God has provided to give direction to my life.
2. Accepting discipline is an important part of my life.
3. When I honor the one God has honored with authority over me, I will be trusted to share in decision-making.
4. How I conduct myself must reveal my faith in God.
5. The consequences of my obedient conduct will be required of me and the one who is over me.

How I conduct myself must reveal my personal faith in God.

Think about the conflict you described earlier. If you are the subordinate in that situation, how should you handle the conflict, using the five-step solution in day 3?

_____

_____

_____

_____

Conflict requires prayerful attention and calls for decisions. As you work to resolve conflicts, keep in mind that the result of all conflict, handled properly, is that we share God's holiness.

End this week's study by writing your Scripture verses.

_____

_____

_____

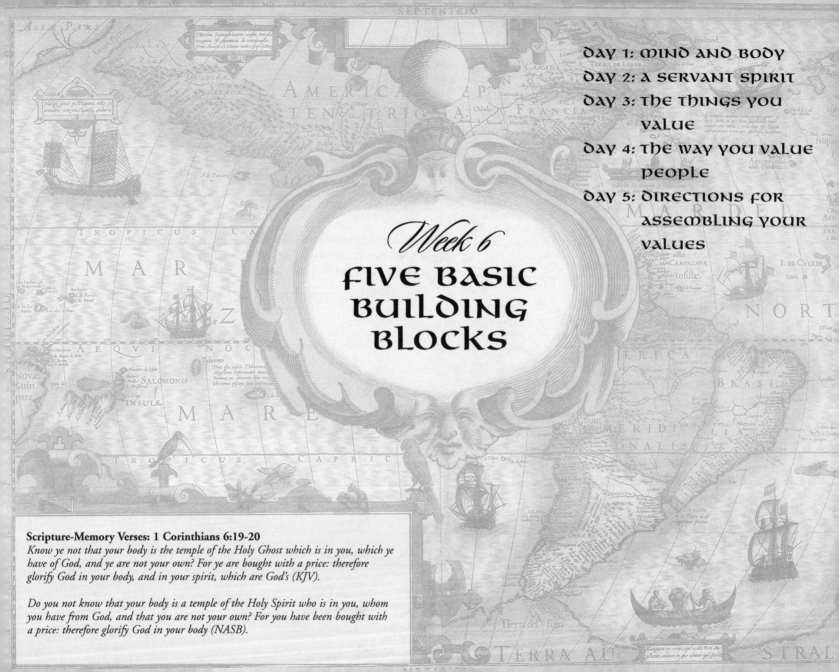

DAY 1: MIND AND BODY

DAY 2: A SERVANT SPIRIT

DAY 3: THE THINGS YOU VALUE

DAY 4: THE WAY YOU VALUE PEOPLE

DAY 5: DIRECTIONS FOR ASSEMBLING YOUR VALUES

Week 6

FIVE BASIC BUILDING BLOCKS

Scripture-Memory Verses: 1 Corinthians 6:19-20

Know ye not that your body is the temple of the Holy Ghost which is in you, which ye have of God, and ye are not your own? For ye are bought with a price: therefore glorify God in your body, and in your spirit, which are God's (KJV).

Do you not know that your body is a temple of the Holy Spirit who is in you, whom you have from God, and that you are not your own? For you have been bought with a price: therefore glorify God in your body (NASB).

Day 1

MIND AND BODY

Use your Scripture-memory card to begin memorizing 1 Corinthians 6:19-20.

You have one more week in *Living Your Christian Values*. Let's review what you've learned about becoming a true minister of God. Fill in the blank fingers in figure 27; then look at what's on the last finger.

Did you write: *One Source of Significance, Two Views of Wealth, Three Necessary Relationships, Four Sources of Conflict?*

During this study we have shaped a few key Christian values. This week you will learn basic truths for shaping all the rest. Five building blocks are available to you in constructing Christian values. Three of these are inside you: your mind and its belief system, your body and the moral use of it as God's temple, and your spirit as a servant of God. Two of them are outside you: the things you consider important and the people in your life.

The first building block you will examine is your mind and its belief system. Do you value your relationship with God more than anything else in life?

Read Matthew 22:37-38.

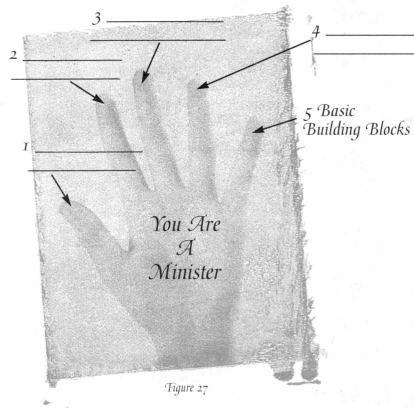

3 _____
_____

2 _____
_____

4 _____
_____

5 Basic Building Blocks

1 _____

You Are A Minister

Figure 27

With what are you to love God?

_____, _____, and _____

How much of each of these three parts of you does God require? _____

Your answers should be: *heart, soul, mind, all.* God wants all of you!

95

The level of your belief in and commitment to God is indicated by the degree to which you incorporate Him into your life moment by moment. Jesus cautioned against allowing our belief system to be shaped by persons who make us feel significant: " 'How can you believe, when you receive glory from one another, and you do not seek the glory that is from the one and only God?' " (John 5:44). If your significance comes from people, your belief in God will be incomplete. If your significance comes completely from being a child of God, your belief in God will be complete.

Focusing on God and seeking Him with the whole heart have always led the seeker to find Him. Write Hebrews 11:6 here.

_____

_____

God rewards those who diligently seek Him. By refusing to seek significance from any source other than God and by seeking Him, your mind will be filled with faith. The first of the five building blocks will then be available!

The second building block for your value system is a Christian view of your body and the moral use of it.

Unbelievers consider the body the most important ingredient of life. For them, a person's worth is revealed by the condition, clothing, transportation, and housing provided for the body. Jesus flatly rejected this whole scheme of things. He wore one seamless robe, never owned a home, disregarded riches, and ridiculed the Pharisees' fixation on finery. He ate whatever He was served. His view of the human body was radically different. Why? He knew that His body was a temporary residence for His eternal life. But something else was far more important: Jesus knew that His body did not house just a human spirit; it also housed the Spirit of the eternal God! Such knowledge changed everything for Him and will change everything for you! Your body is inhabited by the Spirit of God.

Read 1 Corinthians 3:16-17. How do these verses describe the body?

_____

_____

Who dwells in your body (besides you, of course)?

_____

What is the purpose of a temple?

_____

So for what purposes should you use your body?

_____

_____

This passage states that your body is a holy temple in which God's Spirit dwells. Since the purpose of a temple is to provide a place for worship, you should use your body only for purposes that bring pleasure to its owner—God! You do not own your body. You have no right to use it as a means of impressing others with your significance.

Read 1 Corinthians 15:40-49 and 2 Corinthians 6:16—7:1.

The essence of being a slave is that your owner owns everything inside your skin! You have been bought with a price, the precious blood of Jesus Christ. How does accepting this fact change your opinion about certain things you might have done in the past with your body?

List several things you may have done with or to your body before you became a Christian that you would not do now.

_____

_____

Jesus said not to worry about food, clothing, and housing (Matt. 6:25-34). He promised that all things would be provided as you focus on His assignments for your body. Your body is reserved for the exclusive use of its owner, who intends to use it to minister in His name. How does that building block influence your values?

Many Christians faithfully tithe 10 percent of their income and spend the other 90 percent supporting a lavish lifestyle. Does this seem right to you, now that you know who owns your body? Why? Write your answer at the top of the next column.

_____

_____

Describe the kind of lifestyle you should strive to have, considering you are only a steward of your body.

_____

_____

State how this affects your choice of clothes, food, housing, and entertainment.

_____

Touching "what is unclean"—that which defiles the body—involves wrong use of the temple, rather than cherishing it as the temple of the God who inhabits it and valuing the servant ministry it performs (2 Cor. 6:17). Following the admonition of 2 Corinthians 7:1 to "cleanse ourselves from all defilement of flesh" provides another basic building block for all of the values that must be shaped in the future.

Read 1 Corinthians 6:9-18. What does verse 13 say about your body?

_____

_____

By refusing to seek significance from any source other than God and by seeking Him, your mind will be filled with faith.

Your body is not meant for selfish pleasure but to serve the Lord.

From novels to commercials, promiscuity is promoted as a normal and acceptable way of life. The catch words *two consenting adults* provide a "nonmarriage license" for intimacies blessed by the consenters themselves rather than by God. *Adult* implies that if you are of legal age, you have a right to complete freedom. Not so! The body is not the property of its desires, nor are its desires the rights of the body. Paul said, "The body is … for the Lord; and the Lord is for the body." Sexual impurity is a symptom of immaturity and irresponsibility. It is sin—irresponsible self-gratification.

In the Sermon on the Mount (Matt. 5—7), Jesus classified sin into four categories: dishonesty, impurity, self-centeredness, and lack of love. All four of those classifications can be placed under one main title: "How to Live Irresponsibly."

Paul also classified some sins that demonstrate an irresponsible attitude toward God and the life He has so generously given. List the 10 types of sins identified in 1 Corinthians 6:9-10.

1. _____   4. _____

2. _____   5 _____

3. _____   6. _____

7. _____   9. _____

8. _____   10. _____

First Corinthians 6:11 names a solution for all of the sins listed. What is it?

_____

_____

_____

Belief and trust in Jesus Christ washes, sanctifies, and justifies every person who comes to Him repenting! What a relief! No sin on that list will go unforgiven!

Your body is not a temple to be inhabited by dishonesty, impurity, self-centeredness, and lovelessness. First Corinthians 6:19-20 says that it is given to be the temple of God. The ownership of your body has been removed from your control. You no longer dwell alone in your body; you have been indwelled by the King of kings. You did nothing to earn your body, but He gave His body at Calvary to purchase yours!

First Corinthians 6:9-18 explains that you are one with Christ. Faithfulness to Him includes rejecting the use of your body for independent self-gratification that pleases you but brings no delight to Him. Paul stated excellent guidelines for the correct attitude toward using the body.

Read 1 Corinthians 6:9-18. At the top of the next column, match the verse on the left with the guideline it states on the right.

___ 1. Verse 12   a. Sexual impurity is a sin against your own body, God's dwelling place.

___ 2. Verse 13   b. Even though an action may be morally permissible, if it begins to control you rather than your controlling it, it is wrong.

___ 3. Verse 15   c. The body is meant for the service of God's will, not for selfish gratification.

___ 4. Verse 18   d. Your body is a member of the body of Christ.

The answers are *1. b, 2. c, 3. d, 4. a.*

Your body can have no higher purpose than to be Christ's dwelling place. Don't be tricked by Satan into using it for a lower purpose.

Day 2

A SERVANT SPIRIT

Five building blocks are used in constructing your values. Three of these are inside you: your mind and its belief system, your body and the moral use of it, and your spirit as a temple of God. Yesterday you studied mind and body; today you will examine the spirit. A body is like a house. By itself it has no meaning. Its value is created only by the person who inhabits it. The life residing within the body is all that is important.

Read Isaiah 42:5. What does God give to all human beings?

_____ and _____

This verse explains that God gives breath and spirit to all persons. The word spirit refers to the real person, the inner self. God shaped you to be what you are. Your intelligence, your creativity, your talents, and especially your spiritual gifts are His handiwork. You are, as the psalmist said, fearfully and wonderfully made (Ps. 139:14).

Think about your qualities for a moment. Do you realize how unique you are? List several strengths you possess in each of the following areas.

Creativity: _____

_____

Talents: _____

_____

Abilities: _____

_____

Other outstanding characteristics: _____

_____

Your body is not a temple to be inhabited by dishonesty, impurity, self-centeredness, and lovelessness.

99

Can you see that God made you a special person and equipped you with the right qualities and skills to do a specific task for Him? Dedicate your wealth of talent and ability to the use of its owner—God!

Inside your body is you, an eternal spirit. It is important that your spirit be cared for.

Read 2 Corinthians 7:1. What two parts of your being can be defiled?

_____ and _____

Now read 1 Corinthians 7:34. What two parts of you can be holy?

_____ and _____

The answers to both questions are *the body* and *the spirit*! Purity is a word that relates not only to the body but also to the spirit. Your spirit, as well as your body, is God's property. Everything inside your skin belongs to Him!

A reservoir of tremendous power resides in your spirit, just waiting to be released from the confines of the flesh. Through the centuries people have sought to discover how to use that power for their personal profit. Through self-discipline and meditation they have become familiar with the great power that exists in the spirit. Several world religions focus exclusively on the power of the human spirit, rejecting God's existence.

Even within the Christian community some seek to unleash the humans' full potential by rejecting all negative thoughts and the limiting power of the flesh. This approach may teach many positive things, but it makes a person's spirit the exalted center of worship. God's power is seen as a helper to assist people in discovering their own power.

This teaching is very attractive to the human ego, which has always desired to be like God. Unfortunately, the objective is not to bring ultimate glory to God but to celebrate the invincible, unconquerable spirit of humankind. The Book of Romans provides serious problems for those holding this view! Nevertheless, individuals have tremendous potential. Many persons are so crippled by guilt and self-doubt that they never learn what their full capacities could accomplish. When the abilities of the human spirit are released for the work of ministry, God is truly glorified. However, there is a major difference between doing the work of the Lord in the power of the human spirit and doing it in the power of the Holy Spirit. Ephesians 5:18 urges us to "be filled with the Spirit." This newly cleansed spirit of yours must not rely on its own potential but should learn to rely on the power of the Holy Spirit.

Read Acts 4:7-10.

Shortly after Pentecost, Peter and John were imprisoned because of their preaching and healing. They were asked, " 'By what power, or in what name, have you done this?' " Filled with the Holy Spirit, Peter explained that the man stood before them in good health by the power of the name of Jesus Christ. Those disciples spent no time "developing their own potential"; instead, they offered their spirits to be the channel through which God's power might flow. They spent their time enjoying Him, being in union with Him, knowing Him fully. Do the same! Let your spirit belong to Him and let Him control it. Let Him flow His life into your life, His power through your power, His love through your love. Consider your very spirit His servant!

Earlier you considered talents and abilities God has given you, and you dedicated them to His service. Think about how you can also dedicate your spirit to God. Circle the spiritual gifts you feel you possess. Think of two specific ways you can dedicate them to God's use.

encouragement	knowledge
healing	service
giving	wisdom
faith	mercy
teaching	leadership

Two ways to dedicate these gifts:

1. _____

2. _____

A young woman wanted to tell God that she was not her own. Her life had been a sordid one. After learning that she could be adopted by the Master, she prayed: "Lord Jesus, all I know about me I give to all I know about You!"

"All I know about me!" That's a good way to say that you don't know yourself very well, isn't it? Too many values were picked up like germs off the street. Have you ever considered how much is inside you that you don't know about? Maybe you can recall an incident when you did something or reacted in a way that didn't seem like you. Nevertheless, it is important for you to put all of yourself in God's hands—even the parts of yourself you may not be aware of.

"All I know about You!" Our knowledge of God is also limited. The more we know about Him, the deeper our trust and our fellowship become. The process of spiritual maturity is a back-and-forth action in which we know more and more about Him and ourselves, constantly expanding our relationship with Him. The important thing is getting started! Settling once and for all the ownership of your body, mind, and spirit is the starting point of that back-and-forth action. That's why you need to become a slave! Scriptures that refer to us as the slaves of the Father are not too palatable. We shy away from the idea that God is a slave-owner. We envision all slave-owners as cruel. But Paul took pride in the fact that he was God's slave.

Read Romans 1:1; Philippians 1:1 and Titus 1:1. What word did Paul use to describe himself?

_____

He called himself a servant or bond-servant. Paul made no apologies for recognizing that everything inside his skin was the Father's property. He absolutely revoked any claim of ownership over himself. He was a slave.

To fully understand this, let's look at an ancient Jewish custom. Read Deuteronomy 15:12-17.

Dedicate your wealth of talent and ability to the use of its owner—God!

It was an acceptable custom for a person to sell himself into slavery for a period of time. By Jewish law every seventh year was sacred before the Lord, and all slaves were released. Six years, therefore, was the maximum length of service a slave would work for a master. However, someone could enter permanent slavery. After the six years of service had expired, the slave could say: "I love my master. I do not desire to be free. I want to remain voluntarily as a slave."

Having made that decision, the servant would take the lobe of one ear and place it on the edge of a door. The master would take an awl and drive it through the lobe into the door. After the ear lobe had healed, the permanent hole left was a visible sign to all that this person had voluntarily entered slavery! The hole in the ear, therefore, was a tribute to the master's love and concern as well as a mark of the slave's voluntary servanthood.

Do you have a hole in your ear? Christians don't get holes in their ears by accident, but by intentional, deliberate acts of commitment. It is never imposed or demanded by the Master; it is a choice, a voluntary transaction motivated by love. Will there ever be a better time than now? How about using the door of the room you are now in: will it do? Perhaps you would like to stand by it and pray: "Father, all I know about me I give to all I know about You. Signed, Your loving servant with the pierced ear. Amen!"

If you prayed that prayer, write it here as your determination to follow through with your commitment.

_____

_____

_____

_____

_____

_____

_____

_____

Day 3

THE THINGS YOU VALUE

Fill in the diagram of the hand in figure 28.

Thumb: *One Source of Significance*, forefinger: *Two Views of Wealth*, second finger: *Three Necessary Relationships*, third finger: *Four Sources of Conflict*, pinky: *Five Basic Building Blocks.* Now you have a firm grasp on the values of a true minister!

The last two building blocks of your Christian values are outside you: things and people. The fourth building block is the truth that God owns not only everything that is inside your skin but also everything that is outside your skin.

Read Acts 5:1-11.

The family of God was filled with love and fellowship. Every night they ate the evening meal together in the homes of different members. Visiting in homes allowed people to get to know one another and to observe needs of the families they visited. These servant-people also recognized that their property was really the property of their Master; they were merely stewards of His property. It seemed ridiculous for one family to have little when others had much. On a purely voluntary

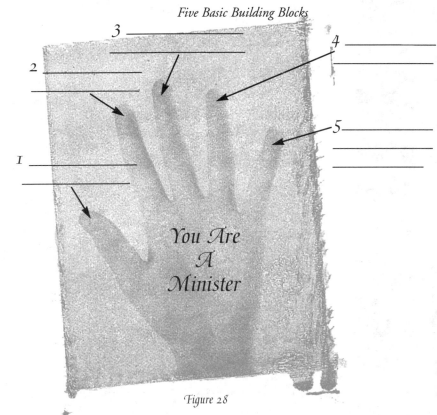

You Are A Minister

Figure 28

basis members of the body sold houses and parcels of land and brought the proceeds to the apostles. The apostles then distributed these proceeds to those in need.

Ananias and his wife, Sapphira, decided to minister this way. However, their treasure chests had some very warped values. From the Scripture passage you just read, can you identify some of these misplaced values?

_____

You may have listed values like the following. *They desired the reputation for being generous people and the respect of the people in their house group. Above all, they wanted to feel the admiring glances of those who would consider them to be significant. To accomplish this, they sold a piece of land and brought the money to the apostles for distribution. Unfortunately, they withheld part of the money for their own use.*

What was so deadly about their mutual decision? First, they loved things more than they loved the family of God. (People who love things usually end up using people.) Second, their act was a statement of their view of things. In their eyes it belonged to them, not to their Master. Third, previous contributions had required real sacrifice by the givers and had not come from the mere surplus of possessions. Fourth, this couple desired to build a reputation to which they had no right.

Describe an occasion when you were tempted to do something good for show and attention.

_____

_____

Explain why this attitude is displeasing to God.

_____

_____

God wants us to find our significance in our relationship with Him, not from the affirmation we get from other people.

Values are not contained by people; they are people! In this case Ananias and Sapphira's values were so twisted that their very presence in the body of Christ was intolerable to the Holy Spirit. Their love for things caused them to pile deceit on lies. In the end their deceit cost them their lives.

What is the lesson for you as you think about building blocks for forming your values? God has promised to provide everything you need. Never hoard your own supply from fear that He may break His promise. The children of Israel were taking baby steps into a walk of faith when they first entered the wilderness. When manna fell from the skies, some decided to hoard private supplies because they did not fully trust God to provide more day by day. Every morsel they hoarded turned sour. Greed still causes things to turn sour! Greed is not a tiny, white-flowered sin. It is a monstrous one that can kill the body or the spirit—or both.

Notice the word *greed* in figure 29. For each letter of the word, write something that begins with that letter that people seek and often value more than they value their relationships with God. The first one is done for you.

G old _____

R _____

E _____

E _____

D _____

Figure 29

No matter what four things you listed, remember that God owns everything; you own nothing! Greed has no place in the life of a true minister!

When God provides you a resource for your ministry to others, never fear that some of it must be retained for yourself. Invest all He supplies; His resources are as endless as your trustworthiness!

Read Luke 16:13-15.

Two masters compete to dominate your life. One is God; the other is riches. Those who love God "hate" riches. Those who love riches "hate" God. There is no room for compromise. Each person is a servant, and each person has only one master.

The Pharisees scoffed at Jesus' words but not because they were wealthy. The amount of a person's wealth has little to do with this issue. Our Lord is perfectly able to be Master of a person whose stewardship includes the use of tens of millions of dollars. Jesus exposed the fact that they lived religious lives on the outside, but in their hearts they didn't love God. They worshiped the god gold. Jesus called attention to their true value system. The building block of God's total ownership of everything did not exist inside them. Life, for them, was bent out of shape. They wanted approval and respect from people, but they didn't want to sacrifice their pleasure to serve God truly. Does this hypocritical attitude remind you of a certain couple you studied recently?

How much money do you think a Pharisee made? Today we would classify them as middle-class. They lived well, but they were not included among the aristocracy. They were not poor, but they had to work for a living every day of their lives except the Sabbath. They could afford no lavish luxuries—just the ordinary kind. But they were lovers of money. They prayed five times a day, tithed, fasted, read their Scriptures, visited prospects—and worshiped money. If it was possible for them, is it possible for you? Is it, in fact, true of you?

Beside each statement write *T* for true or *F* for false.

_____ 1. You don't have to choose between riches and God; you can serve both.

_____ 2. The Pharisees, as a class, were very wealthy.

_____ 3. The Pharisees loved money and prestige more than God.

_____ 4. You can be outwardly religious and inwardly corrupt.

_____ 5. You can love money only if you have a lot of it.

Your answers should be: *1. F, 2. F, 3. T, 4. T, 5. F.*

Stanley Tam is an amazing man. After many years of faithful Christian service he faced a reality in his life. He owned a business that produced hundreds of thousands of dollars of profit, much of which he invested in the Lord's work. One day in the Listening Room God began to speak to him: "Stanley, who owns your business?" "Lord, I do—but You know I use its profit for You." The Father replied: "That's not enough. Transfer the business to Me." Tam informed his lawyer that he wished to transfer all the corporate stock to God and become the employed president of the business rather than the full owner. The lawyer looked at him in amazement and said: "It can't be done; it's unfair to your children; I cannot help you."

Invest all God supplies; His resources are as endless as your trustworthiness!

Stanley Tam found a lawyer who would, and could, legally consummate the transaction. God now literally owns all the stock in that business. As president, Tam draws a sum commensurate with his needs and serves as steward of the corporate dividends, which amount to several million dollars a year. That business venture has sponsored many Christian projects around the world. Only eternity will reveal the tens of thousands who have received Christ because of this one corporation's support of missions.

That story could never have happened if Tam had not used this key building block when selecting every value placed in his treasure chest. The saddest thing about this story is that it is not duplicated by many other successful Christian business persons who both own and operate their businesses.

The amount of income you receive each year has nothing to do with your choice of masters. Your checkbook will not reveal that; your values will! Do you possess this building block? Do you recognize God's ownership of everything outside yourself? You may not be a wealthy business person. You may be poor or just average. Nonetheless, can you show your commitment to trust God with all of your financial dealings?

Think about yourself. Explain how you can live this value of making God the owner of everything outside yourself.

_____

_____

_____

ThE WAY YOU VALUE PEOPLE

Before you begin today's study, review what you've learned so far about building blocks for values. What are the three building blocks that deal with values inside you?

1. _____

2. _____

3. _____

What building block did you study yesterday?

_____

_____

Did you answer values about your mind, body, spirit and the value you place on things?

The fifth building block involves your valued loved ones. They too are included in the realm of everything outside yourself that is owned by God.

Read Genesis 22:1-14.

Isaac was Abraham's miracle baby. For many years he had longed for that son by Sarah. From the moment of his birth Isaac was cherished and loved. Land, tents, cattle, servants, and possessions meant nothing to Abraham. He could have lost his entire fortune without having his faith in God shaken. Isaac, however, was a different matter. Abraham dearly loved his son. To lose him would be to lose his most precious possession of all.

Some have recoiled against this demand God made, saying that it is not consistent with God's loving nature. They miss the point! One way or the other, Isaac was not to die. If Abraham had failed this test of his commitment and faith, he would have refused to offer Isaac. In passing the test, he was given a substitute to offer in Isaac's place. The point of this experience was to help Abraham place in his treasure chest once and for all this fifth building block for shaping his values. Abraham settled with finality the fact that God would forever be first in his life.

Do you need a trip of your own to Moriah's mountain? Have you moved a loved one or loved ones into your throne room? Do you own them, or does God own them? These are hard questions, aren't they? After all, God wants us to love our families and our friends. He wants us to give to them and to sacrifice for them. So how do we know when these persons have become more important to us than God?

To help you develop guidelines for answering his question, write *L* beside each of the following sentences that describes appropriate love and a *W* beside the ones that describe inappropriate worship.

_____ 1. Wade's two-year-old son meant more to him than anything in the world—including his wife, his church, and his family.

_____ 2. Carolyn stopped teaching Sunday School and singing in the choir because her husband wanted her to spend Sunday mornings with him, sleeping late and having a leisurely brunch.

_____ 3. Denise loved her fiance´ so much that she didn't argue when he insisted on having sexual relations before they married.

_____ 4. Tim and Lisa dedicated their six-month-old daughter to the Lord and placed her in His care.

Did you write *1. W, 2. W, 3. W, 4. L*?

God wants us to love our families and our friends.

One Christian worker let his church members know that they could expect him to put his wife and family first at all times. With almost a fierceness he separated his ministry time from his family time. The years passed. Then with a broken heart he watched his children leave home—and leave God. He realized too late what he had done. By putting his family first—before God and his ministry—he had made skeptics of them. They had become convinced by his enthronement of the family that God was not nearly as important as he preached Him to be!

How do you value the people in your life? Have you understood the importance of putting God before every person in every situation? It's important to love God more than the people in your life—and then to model the great depth of your love for both Him and them. It's also important to know that He will not only provide special people for you but will also care for them.

Read 1 Corinthians 7:19-31.

In verses 29-31 Paul spoke from his own value system, urging you to recognize the importance of your ministry and to put it before every person and circumstance in your life. His words reflect the teaching of Jesus, who instructed us to "let the dead bury their dead" (Matt. 8:22, KJV) and informed those who loved relatives more than Him that they were not worthy of Him.

What guidelines can you use to help you decide when you're putting your love for another person before your love for God? Write them here.

_____

_____

You may have included such thoughts as: Never break a commandment or go against the teachings of the Bible for the sake of a loved one; never become so attached to human beings that you'd do anything, including disobeying God, to protect them or make them happy.

God is the creator of all the special people in your life. He gave them to you. But they must never become more important to you than He is or more important than your ministry as a servant-priest. This building block has another dimension:

which people do you value? Do you consider your blood family more significant than the family of God?

Read Matthew 12:46-50.

Jesus was interrupted one day while He was teaching. "Behold, Your mother and Your brothers are standing outside seeking to speak to You." This person assumed that Jesus accepted this value and would immediately dismiss the crowd to talk to His family. In response Jesus asked, " 'Who is My mother and who are My brothers?' " He swept His hand to indicate the crowd of disciples and said: " 'Behold, My mother and My brothers! For whoever does the will of My Father who is in heaven, he is My brother and sister and mother.' "

State in your own words what Jesus was saying.

_____

_____

_____

_____

_____

You may have expressed it differently, but Jesus' main idea is that our brothers and sisters in Christ are just as important as our blood relatives—including the most intimate family ties of mother, father, brother, and sister. When you become a child of God, you become part of God's family!

Describe the obligations and sharing of resources that take place among those who are related by blood. What kinds of giving do you do for your family members?

_____

_____

_____

You may have listed such things as caring for your elderly parents, sharing financial resources with a brother or a sister who is out of work, taking care of your nieces and nephews so your brother or sister can rest, and so on.

Now think about it: Would you do the same for your brother or sister in Christ? Would you feel obligated to help them? ❏ Yes ❏ No If not, you need to rethink this value and replace it with the one Christ modeled for us in Matthew 12:46-50.

It is absurd to think that blood-family relationships will be destroyed by accepting your brothers and sisters in Christ as equal in importance. The opposite is true! Self-centered relationships will be replaced by an awareness that every person has worth, not just some persons. Ministry is changed from a personal assignment to a family assignment. Children learn to love and care by observing parents who do not limit their affection to members of their human family. Also the watching world of skeptics begins to see the radical life of Christians who take seriously their relationships with others.

In one church a group of teenagers became aware of a family desperately in need of $1,800. Within a week's time they earned nearly $185 to help with the crisis. The mother, not yet a Christian, was overwhelmed by their gesture. Six months later the church received large checks at Christmastime from two corporations that had heard about the teenagers' gift. When asked how the money was to be spent, one executive said: "We don't care how you spend it! People like you don't have to be told how to spend money. You really are the family of God."

God owns everything and everyone, and that includes your family.

This building block contains the same truth that shaped the first four: God owns everything and everyone, and that includes your family. It also means that His family is as precious as your family, and you cannot single out one over the other to receive greater attention. Love the body of Christ! Jesus did—enough to give His life for it.

Make a commitment to be aware of the needs of your brothers and sisters in Christ. The next time you see a need, ask yourself, What would I do if that person were my father or mother? Then do it! You may want to write your commitment here.

_____

_____

_____

_____

Day 5

DIRECTIONS FOR ASSEMBLING YOUR VALUES

It is not the application of Christian values that leads to Christ. Instead, a personal encounter with Christ transforms lives and helps persons shape Christian values for living. Do not substitute a system of Christian ethics for a personal, intimate relationship with your Master. The Jews in Jesus' day made that error, and it led them into spiritual decay. The Spirit of Christ does not lead you by giving rules but by giving Himself to you. Communion with Him takes place in the Listening Room of your life. Use God's written Word to study the way He guided other servants in other places. You will never face a situation that someone in Scripture has not already faced. God's directions to them are still valid.

One goal of this study has been to help you love and respect your Bible as God's guidebook for shaping values. Day after day you have discovered new truths in the Old Testament and in the New Testament. On a few occasions during this study certain Scripture passages were deliberately used more than once, providing counsel for different situations. The Scriptures became alive all over again, didn't they? Although the application was new, the truth of the passage did not change.

Above all, remember that the most important thing in your existence is your servant-priest ministry for your Master. He owns you and your family, along with all of the possessions that surround you. Expect to do mighty things for Him, using His power—not yours! Remember where you will find Him— at the side of a hurting person, not in a tranquil room that insulates you from the needs of Adam's children.

Matthew 5—7 contains your directions for assembling all values! You can use this passage to shape your values through the rest of your life.

Amazingly, Jesus said virtually all He had to say about Christian values in this one address. Jesus took 20 minutes to present it and then spent 3 years modeling it before His disciples. Do you realize that this passage is the only record of any sermon Jesus ever preached? Surely that reveals how important the message is. Saturate your mind with its teachings.

Spend several weeks studying Matthew 5—7. Ponder Jesus' comments about judgmentalism, hatred, and murder. Consider His teachings about adultery, divorce, oaths, and retaliation. Meditate on the text of the prayer given to the disciples, which is reserved for the exclusive use of Jesus' slaves. At the end of the sermon ponder the metaphors about the two roads, the two fruits, and the two builders.

Your daily time with your Lord in the Listening Room must become a lifelong activity. As long as you are a servant, you will find it necessary to hear the voice of your Master.

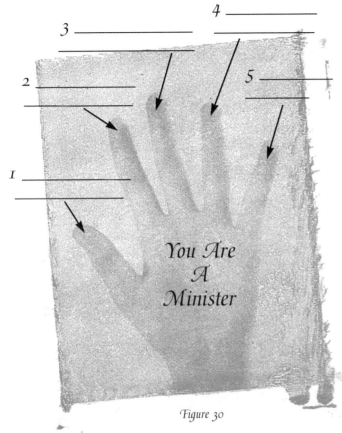

3 _____

4 _____ _____

2 _____

5 _____

1 _____

You Are A Minister

Figure 30

This brings us to the end of this six-week spiritual journey. Let's review this week's memory verses. Write them below.

_____

_____

Let's review the outline of our study. By this time, you understand what to do with figure 30, don't you?

Now take time to assess the effect this study has had on your life. The purposes of this spiritual journey have been to help you recognize your values and to help you reshape them into the values of a true minister.

How well do you know your values now?

Very Well		Somewhat Well		Still Unsure
1	2	3	4	5

Are your values more in line with what God desires than they were six weeks ago?

Much More		Somewhat More		Not a Bit More
1	2	3	4	5

In which area of your life have your values changed most? Explain.

_____

_____

_____

Which values still need more reshaping to make them pleasing to God?

Your daily time with your Lord in the Listening Room must become a lifelong activity.

Thoughtfully review your life for the past six weeks. What have been your greatest victories in your spiritual journey?

_____

_____

_____

_____

_____

Your greatest setbacks?

_____

_____

_____

_____

Stop and thank God for both. Pray especially that He will continue to use both victories and setbacks to reshape your life in His image.

Now for a final word: Welcome, my friend, to the rest of your life. The other limbs and members of the body welcome your ministry to them and with them. Even the gates of hell cannot prevail against you! Glory be to God!

James E. Taulman

Leader Guide

INTRODUCTORY SESSION

Session goal: After this session members will have introduced themselves, overviewed the topics in *Living Your Christian Values,* and received instructions for completing the study.

Preparing to Lead the Session

1. At least four weeks in advance order copies of *Living Your Christian Values.* You can purchase these by writing Customer Service Center, MSN 113; 127 Ninth Avenue, North; Nashville, TN 37234-0113; faxing (615) 251-5933; calling (800) 458-2772; ordering online at http://www.lifeway.com; emailing customerservice@lifeway.com; or visiting a LifeWay Christian Store.
2. Arrange a table with material for members to use to make name tags.
3. Place a registration form on each chair.
4. Make a course poster by drawing a large outline of the hand shown on page 5. Write on the poster: *You are a minister.* Be prepared to write the title of each group session on the appropriate finger as you begin that week's session. Place the poster on the wall before each session.
5. Arrange chairs in a circle before each session.

6. On an 8½-by-11 sheet of paper, record the following instructions: *Write your name vertically down the left side of the paper. Form an acrostic by using the letters of your name to write characteristics about yourself. Below the acrostic write in one sentence what you want to gain from this study.* Place a copy of this get-acquainted activity on each chair.
7. Prepare slips of paper with one of the following words or phrases written on each: *minister, God, wealth, relationships, conflict, building blocks.*
8. Have felt-tip pens and large sheets of paper taped to the wall for use during the session.
9. For each session have quiet, inspirational music playing as members arrive. Turn the music off when you begin.

Leading the Session

1. As members arrive, ask them to prepare name tags reflecting their personalities and/or Christian lives.
2. Ask members to complete the registration form and the get-acquainted activity.
3. Collect registration forms and call on several to share their acrostic. Ask members to read aloud what they want to gain from the study.
4. Distribute copies of *Living Your Christian Values.* Explain the format of the study. Ask them to complete week 1 before the next session. Point out the Scripture-memory cards at the center of the book and encourage members to memorize the suggested verses each week.
5. Invite members to play a game that will introduce the next six sessions. Tell them that you will give six of them a word, and you want them to draw something that represents that word on one of the large sheets of paper on the wall. Then the group will guess what the word is.

Distribute the slips of paper you prepared. Allow two minutes for each word. If fewer than six persons are in the group, assign more than one word to some members until all six words are assigned.

6. After each word is guessed or a one-minute period is over, share what that word means to the study.

7. Divide the group into small groups of three or four. If fewer than six are in your group, do not divide the group. Ask each member to answer the following questions: Where did you live between the ages of 7 and 12? How did you heat your home during this period? What was the emotional center of warmth in your home? When did God become more than just a word to you? Let each person respond before asking the next question.

8. When all have shared, ask members to join hands and pray sentence prayers for one another.

9. As members leave, encourage them to complete their studies for next week.

Developing your value system

Session goal: After this session members will be able to describe steps for developing their value systems.

Preparing to Lead the Session

1. Provide an envelope and a slip of paper for each member. Number the envelopes consecutively with a small number in the upper left-hand corner.

2. Write Ephesians 4:31-32 on a large sheet of paper, leaving blanks in place of a few strategic words. Place this poster on the focal wall. Write the words that go in the blanks on strips of paper. Have tape available to fasten the word strips to the poster.

3. Write each of the following three words on 8½-by-11 sheets of paper and tape one in three different corners of the room: *people, emotions, habits.* Tape a large sheet of paper and a felt-tip pen on the wall below each word.

4. Prepare a poster: *If you do not examine your old values, you will become like them!*

5. Provide paper and a pencil for each member.

6. Draw a picture of a ranch-style house with trees and flowers. Keep the drawing simple.

Leading the Session

1. As members enter, give them the word strips that complete the poster of Ephesians 4:31-32. Ask them to be prepared later to place their words in the proper places. When all have arrived, ask them where they have seen these verses this week. (*their memory verses*) Ask members to place their words in the proper positions. When the poster is complete, read the verse aloud. Then let volunteers repeat it from memory. Encourage members to memorize the suggested verses each week.

2. Call attention to the poster that reads, *If you do not examine your old values, you will become like them!* Review the way values are haphazardly collected. Point out that believers need to intentionally select values that honor God.

3. Divide members into three groups. Assign each group one of the three words taped to the wall. Ask the groups to go to their words, identify values they have received from that particular source, and write them on the large sheet beneath the word. Ask the groups to share their ideas with all members. Ask each group to write *N* (new self) beside values a Christian should possess and *O* (old self) beside values that seem questionable for a Christian.

4. Distribute paper and a pencil to each member. Divide the group in half. Ask each person to draw a picture of a house with trees and flowers. However, show your picture to half of the group and ask them to draw a house just like yours. When all have finished their drawings, ask them to hold them up for the group to see. Ask the group that did not see your picture why their pictures do not look like yours. Point out that it is hard to do what is required without a proper model. Let the group suggest why it is necessary for

Christians to choose proper models. Point out that the best model is Jesus. We have several sources that help us understand what Jesus wants from us. Ask members to recall these resources from their study this week. Write them on the chalkboard or on a large sheet of paper. (See the activity on page 15 for suggestions.)

5. Read the following case study: Sue liked her new job. One day her manager came by and complimented her on her work. He made some veiled references to her "cooperating" with him so that she could move up in the company. If she did not go along with him, he assured her that she would not receive a promotion. Having just graduated from college, Sue had loans to pay and really needed the job. She thought for a while and said …

6. Let members respond. Ask whether being a Christian would influence their response. Say, Satan can use emotions, feelings, and desires as entry points in our daily living. There are two other entry points. Ask the group to name the other two. (*Habits and patterns of your old lifestyle, your mind*)

7. Divide the group in half. Ask one half to write a brief case study illustrating the way Satan can use habits and patterns of our old lifestyle as an entry point into our lives. Ask the other half to write a case study illustrating the way Satan can use our minds as an entry point. Let each group read its case study to the whole group.

8. Ask members to share the two things they listed in the activity in week 1 on page 18 that tell what Paul did to show his commitment. Then let them share the commitments they will make.

9. Give each person an envelope and a piece of paper. Ask members to write their names and phone numbers on the

paper and to place it in the envelope and seal it, noting the small number in the upper left-hand corner. Collect the envelopes and distribute them to the group. (Be sure members do not get their own numbers.) Ask them to open the envelope when they get home and place the person's name in a prominent place. Instruct them to pray each day that the person will be able to weed out inadequate values and replace them with values that would please God. Ask each member to call the person the day before the next session and let him know he had been prayed for during the week.

10. Close by praying that God will grant wisdom to help members formulate new values.

ONE SOURCE OF SIGNIFICANCE

Session goal: After this session members will be able to identify God as the one source of their significance and to name the way God's children become significant.

Preparing to Lead the Session

1. Place the course poster on the wall. You will add *One Source of Significance* during the session.
2. Make a strip poster: *Attempting to earn acceptance and love is the hallmark of the behavior of Adam's children.* Place this on the focal wall.
3. Secure paper, pencils, and a small, metal container such as a trash can.
4. Write the following questions on strips of colored paper. *What makes us special in God's sight? How do most people feel they can achieve significance? What does it mean to be made in God's image? What are some characteristics we share with God? What is the problem with trying to earn our significance?* Write the answers to the questions on strips of paper of another color: *We are created in His image. By earning their significance. To share some of God's characteristics. The ability to create and the capacity to love. We never achieve enough.*

5. Write the word *servant* down the left side of a large sheet of paper or on the chalkboard.
6. Tape three large sheets of paper and felt-tip pens to the wall in different areas of the room.
7. Be sure everyone has a Bible. Different translations will help.
8. Prepare a strip poster that lists the following sentences. Cover the sentences until you are ready to use them. *You are significant because you are God's child. Because you don't prove significance by what you do, you are free. Your freedom permits you to become a servant of all. As a servant, you can invest your life in meaningful, rather than self-centered, activity. Being a minister, no matter how costly, is the highest way to use your life!*

Leading the Session
1. Read the following case study: Sarah had grown up in poverty with an alcoholic father who often abused her. But she escaped her surroundings and eventually became a successful lawyer. However, one calm summer night she went home and committed suicide. Why would someone with everything going for her do this? Say, This week's study explained what makes us significant.
2. Play "Answers and Questions." The goal is to match questions with answers. Distribute answers to 5 group members and questions to 5 other members. Let members with the answers read them and see whether the person with the right questions can match them. If the group has fewer than 10 members, give more than one strip to a person.
3. Call attention to the strip poster that reads, *Attempting to earn acceptance and love is the hallmark of the behavior of Adam's children.* Ask members if they agree or disagree

with the statement. Point to the course poster and write *One Source of Significance* on it. Let a volunteer suggest what our one source of significance is and why.
4. Ask members to work in pairs to answer the question: Why do our attempts to earn our significance always end in failure? Give paper and pencils to each pair. Say, List as many reasons as you can why this is true and share them with the group.
5. Point out that if we cannot gain significance by earning it, we have to look for meaning someplace else. Ask a volunteer to read Ephesians 5:1-2. Ask, What two actions are we to perform because we are God's children? (*be like God, walk in love*) How do these two actions add meaning to life?
6. Distribute paper and pencils. Ask members to bow their heads. Read Philippians 3:7-8. Ask members whether, because they are God's children, they need to count something as loss for Christ. If so, ask them to write it on a piece of paper and walk to the metal container, tear up the paper, and drop it in. After all have finished, lead in a prayer of thanksgiving and commitment.
7. Form three small groups and ask each group to write on a large sheet of paper a definition of *servant*. Let the groups share their definitions.
8. Call attention to the word *servant*. Ask the group to suggest a word or phrase that begins with each letter and can be used to describe a servant. Write the words or phrases on the large sheet of paper or on the chalkboard. Ask each member to choose the word or phrase that describes the quality he or she most needs to work on.
9. Ask members to form small groups of three. Ask half of the groups to turn to Matthew 16:25 and the other half to

Romans 11:33—12:2 and to (1) write a paraphrase of the Scripture and (2) tell why the verses are significant to Christian servanthood.

10. Ask a volunteer to read John 12:25-26. Ask members what this passage means. Allow time for responses. Uncover the statements on the strip poster and comment on each.

11. Distribute pencils and paper. Call attention to the following sentence on page 35: "There is a huge difference between praying, 'Lord, please bless what I'm doing' and 'Lord, let me do what You're blessing!' " Ask members to choose one area of their lives in which they attempt to serve Christ and write that on the sheet of paper, replacing the word *do* in the above sentence with their activity. Ask them to turn to another member and share: (1) what they wrote and why and (2) how doing what they have written would help them present their bodies as living sacrifices to God.

12. Ask a volunteer to read Luke 14:26-27. Discuss what it means to bear a cross.

13. Close by praying that members will find their source of significance in God.

Session 3

TWO VIEWS OF WEALTH

Session goal: After this session members will be able to identify two views of wealth, summarize the fallacy of the human-centered view of wealth, and demonstrate an understanding that all wealth is controlled by God.

Preparing to Lead the Session

1. Write the following paragraph on a sheet of paper, omitting the underlined letters, and make a copy for each member. *This short paragraph contains one of the greatest statements regarding wealth which God has given to His children. Looking at it from a human perspective, it doesn't make sense. However, acknowledging this affirmation allows believers to catch a vision of what wealth can accomplish when surrendered to God.*

2. Make a poster of the following and place it on a focal wall. Cover each line until you use it.
   Two Views of Wealth
   • *People Control Wealth*
   • *God Controls Wealth*

3. Prepare copies of the following group assignments. *Group 1*—Read Luke 12:16-19. Identify all of the ways the man in the parable demonstrated that he followed the philosophy that people control wealth. *Group 2*—Read Luke

12:16-19. Identify what changes the man in the parable would have had to make to begin believing that God controls wealth.

4. Display the course poster; add *Two Views of Wealth*.

5. Write the following questions on a large poster titled *Transferable Wealth: After earthly treasures have been passed from generation to generation, what finally happens to them? Will any treasure on earth last forever? In light of this, what should a Christian consider to be profitable in this life?* Cover the questions with strips of adding-machine tape.

6. Provide pencils and paper.

7. Make the following poster.
   Four Characteristics of a Fully-Committed Servant
   • *Servanthood has ended the search for significance.*
   • *The servant's assignment is to do the work of a steward.*
   • *No compromise is in this servant's heart.*
   • *There is a special compassion for those who are "blind."*

8. Prepare a banner that says: *Learn to live simply so that others may simply live.*

Leading the Session

1. As members enter, give them copies of the paragraph with the letters omitted and ask them to supply the missing letters to complete the words in the paragraph. Then ask them to use the letters they added to make a Scripture verse. ("The earth is the Lord's, and all it contains" [1 Cor. 10:26]). When members have finished, read the Scripture and call attention to the course poster.

2. Call attention to the poster identifying two views of wealth. Ask members to recall the two views of wealth. Uncover each view as it is named.

3. Divide the group in half and give out the assignments you prepared in advance. Ask the groups to complete their assignments and report.

4. Invite members to answer as you uncover each question on the poster *Transferable Wealth*.

5. With members still in two groups, make the following assignments. *Group 1*—Read 1 Thessalonians 5:2-3; 2 Peter 3:7-10. *Group 2*—Read 1 Thessalonians 5:6; 2 Peter 3:11-13. Ask each group to decide on a one-sentence summary of these verses and to present this summary to the larger group.

6. Give members pencils and paper and ask them to draw a line down the center of the paper. To help members determine if their actions indicate whether their values reflect the kingdom of the world or the kingdom of God, ask them to write on one side of the paper all the evidence that their values reflect the kingdom of this world. On the other side of the paper, list all the evidence that their values reflect the kingdom of God. When they have finished their lists, remind them that they were to examine their checkbooks this week to see what they revealed about their wealth. Ask, In light of what you have discovered about your values, do you need to make any changes in your values toward wealth?

7. Ask the group to turn the paper over and answer the question, What do you have that will transfer from this world to the next?

8. Read the contract on page 47. Ask: How did you feel about signing this contract? What made you want to do it? Do you believe that God will take care of you? Ask whether any members had reservations about signing it.

9. Call attention to the poster *Four Characteristics of a Fully-Committed Servant.* Ask members to share how important they feel these characteristics are. Ask volunteers to share how they ranked themselves on each rating scale on pages 48-49.

10. Display the banner that reads, *Learn to live simply so that others may simply live.* Ask members to discuss in pairs what this statement means. Ask them to consider these questions: How much is enough? What are my rights as a Christian to spend money I earn legitimately in any way I wish that is morally right? After members have discussed these points, ask them to share any insights they have gained.

11. Call for members' responses to the questions on page 53. Ask, How did answering these questions make you feel?

12. Close by praying that members will acknowledge God's ownership of all wealth and that they will willingly offer Him their wealth for His use.

Session 4

THREE NECESSARY RELATIONSHIPS

Session goal: After this session members will be able to describe how they should relate to God, believers, and unbelievers.

Preparing to Lead the Session

1. Display the course poster and add *Three Necessary Relationships.*

2. Make a poster that reads: *A ritual practice of religion can never substitute for a life of righteousness or for serving and ministering to others.*

3. Make a copy of these role-play situations: Group 1—A sick friend needs to be taken to the doctor. You tell her you can't take her because you are on your way to your prayer group but that you will request prayer for her. Group 2—A friend who is going through a divorce calls as you are going out the door on your way to church visitation. You tell him you don't have time to talk. Group 3—You are asked to help distribute clothing at a homeless shelter, but you have to go to your Bible-study group.

4. Have available a large sheet of paper. Provide paper, pencils, and envelopes for all members.

5. Make copies of the following choral reading from Romans 12:9-16, GNB, for all members. Enlist two members to be readers 1 and 2.

All: Love must be completely sincere.

Reader 1: Hate what is evil,

Reader 2: hold on to what is good.

All: Love one another warmly as Christian brothers,

Reader 1: and be eager to show respect for one another.

Reader 2: Work hard and do not be lazy.

Reader 1: Serve the Lord with a heart of devotion.

All: Let your hope keep you joyful,

Reader 1: be patient in your troubles,

Reader 2: and pray at all times.

Reader 1: Share your belongings with your needy   fellow Christians,

Reader 2: and open your homes to strangers.

All: Ask God to bless those who persecute you—

Reader 1: yes, ask Him to bless,

Reader 2: not to curse.

All: Be happy with those who are happy, weep with those who weep.

Reader 1: Have the same concern for everyone.

Reader 2: Do not be proud,

Reader 1: but accept humble duties.

All: Do not think of yourselves as wise.

Leading the Session

1. State that because members are more than halfway through the study, you want to check their Scripture memorization. Call out a word or phrase from each memory verse members have learned to this point and invite them to quote the verse and reference:

malice (Eph. 4:31-32), *transformed* (Rom. 12:1-2), *treasures* (Matt. 6:19-21), *love of God* (Rom. 8:38-39).

2. Call attention to the course poster. Point out the inscription on the third finger. Ask: What relationships have you studied this week? (*relating to God, believers, and unbelievers*)

3. Ask: Based on your study this week, how should you relate to God? (*enjoy Him forever*) Why should you enjoy God? (*He owns the world, has fellowship with His people, provides for our needs, protects, and disciplines.*)

4. State that we need not be afraid to do what God has called us to do. Ask members to discuss with a partner: Why are we afraid? (*many reasons such as previous experiences in childhood and adulthood, but a lack of faith in God to care for us underlies these.*) How can we eliminate fear? (*admit our fears, examine our fears, pray, but most importantly, trust God to care for us and protect us*)

5. Ask, How does the Listening Room help us understand God's will? Invite members to list ways God reveals His will. (*study or read the Bible, pay attention to opportunities as they arise, be aware of strong feelings, get counsel*)

6. Ask, What is the final authority for determining whether God or someone else is speaking? (*the Bible*) Ask members to turn to page 62 and underline this sentence: "In fact, this written Word is so important that you may be absolutely certain about this: no person ever receives another word from God that is not in harmony with the Bible."

7. Call attention to the banner. Divide into three groups and give each group one of the role-play situations. Allow the groups two minutes to select and review their roles. Then call for the role plays to be enacted. Remind the group

that while prayer, visitation, and Bible study are necessary, they must not become ends in themselves. Jesus will always be where people need ministry.

8. Point out that individually we cannot do all of the ministry the church can accomplish by working together. We need other Christians, and they need us. Distribute copies and lead the group through the choral reading of Romans 12:9-16, GNB.

9. Ask members to think of one ministry suggested by Romans 12:9-16 they would like to have received. Distribute pieces of paper and ask them to write the ministries and their names. Fold the pieces of paper and collect them. Place the pieces of paper in a basket and let each person select one. Ask members to do their best to perform the ministry to that person.

10. Distribute envelopes and ask members to write their names on the envelopes. Distribute as many pieces of paper to each person as you have members present. Ask members to write on a separate piece of paper a special talent or gift possessed by each member. When all have finished, members should pass the envelopes as they place in each envelope what they have written about that person.

11. Ask, What symbol of our relationship with Jesus do we share with all believers? (*the Lord's Supper*) Call attention to the true/false exercise about the Lord's Supper on page 70. Discuss responses and make sure all members are clear on these points.

12. Explain that not only do we relate to the body, but we also relate to Adam's children. Ask members to turn to page 71 and underline the sentence: "Yet, your presence among those who do not know Christ is at the very heart of your work as a minister." Ask several members to share what this statement implies about their relationships in the world.

13. Ask a volunteer to read Romans 10:12-15. Ask members to suggest the two factors involved in every unbeliever's conversion. (*hearing the good news and responding to the good news*) Write these on the chalkboard or on a large sheet of paper. Ask, Which of these is our responsibility? (*speaking the good news so that people hear*) Read the case study about John on page 72. Ask, How does this case study make you feel? If you don't become God's minister to the lost, who will take your place?

14. Close by praying that members will relate properly to God, believers, and unbelievers.

four sources of conflict

Session goal: After this session members will be able to identify four sources of conflict, ways these conflicts affect their daily lives, and ways they can overcome these conflicts.

Preparing to Lead the Session
1. Display the course poster and add *Four Sources of Conflict.*
2. Prepare a poster of the four sources of conflict: *Conflict Inside Yourself, Conflict with Someone Else, Conflict Because of Your Convictions, Conflict Between Authority and Responsibility.* Cover each line and place the poster on the wall.
3. Enlist two members to help you in a role play. Instruct them not to let anyone know you have asked them to help. Arrange the chairs in a semicircle. Place two chairs at the top of the semicircle. Use one of the chairs for yourself. When you ask the members to form groups of three, have the two enlisted members begin arguing over who is going to sit in a particular chair (*conflict with someone else*). One person should insist that you asked him or her to sit there (*conflict over authority and responsibility*), and therefore he or she should sit in the chair (*conflict because of your convictions*). Have them start in low voices, just talking about the problem. Have them build to a volume where everyone in the room is listening and feeling uncomfortable

(*conflict inside yourself*). This should take less than two minutes.
4. Write on a piece of paper: *Repeat this week's memory verses to the group.* Place the paper in an envelope and tape it under one chair in the room.

Leading the Session
1. Ask members to look under their chairs to find the envelope you taped there. The person who finds it should recite this week's memory verses. Encourage members to keep working on their memory verses.
2. Ask members to divide into groups of three. As members begin moving, this is the signal for the two enlisted persons to begin their role play. When the role play is completed, interrupt and ask members what they are feeling. Ask the two who did the role play to share their feelings, too. Uncover the first point on the session poster, *Conflict Inside Yourself.* Ask how many felt conflict during the role play. Identify the other three types of conflict.
3. Say, Assume that the role play was a real conflict between two persons. Ask, Is it accurate to say that the source of the conflict was their desire to be significant? How important is it to save face?
4. Ask someone to briefly summarize Peter's conflict in Acts 10:1-16.
5. Address the second point on the poster. Remind members that they studied a four-step plan for resolving conflict with someone else. Ask members to turn to Matthew 5:23-24; 18:16-17 and suggest what the two role-play participants should do to try to resolve their conflict. (*one should talk to the other, two witnesses, the whole body, treat the offending member like a Gentile*)

6. Review the five lessons on pages 85-86 for dealing with conflict with someone else. Ask members to share how they resolved the conflict in the case study on page 86.

7. Write *7 x 70 = 490* on a sheet of paper. Ask members what this equation means and how they can apply it to their lives. (See Matt. 18:21-22.)

8. Point to the third type of conflict on the poster, *conflict because of your convictions*. Ask members to respond to the following case study: Susan moved to a community dominated by a particular religion. She opened a store, and all of the local townspeople started trading there. They all ran up large charge accounts. One day representatives of the religion visited Susan and asked her to join their church. When Susan explained that she was already an active member of her church and did not want to change, she was told that she had two choices: either convert to their religion or face bankruptcy because they would instruct their members who owed money not to pay their bills. Susan said ...[1]

9. Ask members whether they agree or disagree with this statement: "Any conviction you would be willing to compromise is not a true value!" Ask, Why do people act one way in front of one group of people and another way in front of a different group of people? How can we develop values that help us obey God regardless of the cost? How can we eliminate the inner struggle over whether we should participate in an activity that is less than Christ-like? How can our hypocrisy and lack of consistency in the midst of conflict hurt other people?

10. Call attention to the fourth source of conflict on the poster *conflict between authority and responsibility*. Divide the group in half. Ask one group to identify a principle that can help them resolve conflict between someone in authority over them. *(love for each other causes each person to give and receive responsibility and authority in the relationship)* Ask the other group to identify a principle that can help them resolve conflict with a person equal in authority. *(show positive, redemptive actions in a spirit of patience and a desire to do good for the other person)* Let groups share their principles.

11. Invite someone to read Hebrews 12:14. Say, Conflict helps us mature as Christians.

12. Close by praying that God will use the conflicts in members' lives to help them mature.

Session 6

FIVE BASIC BUILDING BLOCKS

Session goal: After this session members will be able to identify three internal and two external building blocks they can use to shape their values in the future.

Preparing to Lead the Session

1. Display the course poster and add *Five Basic Building Blocks*.
2. Write each memory verse on a separate strip of paper. Make enough strips for each member to have one.
3. Prepare a session poster titled *Five Basic Building Blocks*. List the following: *Your Mind and Its Belief System, Your Body and the Moral Use of It as God's Temple, Your Spirit as a Servant of God, Things Considered Important in Your Life, The People Who Surround Your Life.*
4. Provide a three-by-five-inch card and a straight pin or piece of tape for each member, paper and pencils, a chalkboard or a large sheet of paper, and an awl.
5. Write these questions on a large sheet of paper: *In which area of your life have your values changed the most? Which values still need the most reshaping to make them pleasing to God? What have been your greatest victories in your spiritual journey? What have been your greatest setbacks in your spiritual journey?* Display on a focal wall.

Leading the Session

1. As each member enters, pin or tape one of the memory-verse strips on the person's back. Instruct members to guess what the verse is by asking no more than one question of one other person. When they have guessed the verse, they must repeat it to the person, who checks the recitation for accuracy.
2. Call attention to the course poster and state that this is the final session of study. Help members briefly review the topics written on each finger of the poster.
3. Call attention to the session poster and remind members of the five building blocks.
4. Ask members to work in pairs to answer the question, How do I determine whether God is real in my life? After about three minutes, ask them to share their answers with the group. Write these on the chalkboard or on a large sheet of paper. Examine the ideas suggested and then ask members how they can incorporate any of these suggestions into their lives to help them feel that God is real.
5. Point to *Your Mind and Its Belief System* on the session poster. Ask, How does this building block influence your life? Allow time for response.
6. Point out the second building block on the session poster: *Your Body and the Moral Use of It as God's Temple.* Divide into two groups. Ask group 1 to identify the positive aspects of the second building block and to answer, What does this building block require me to do with my life? Ask group 2 to identify the negative aspects of the second building block and to answer, What does this building block prohibit from my life? Allow three or four minutes for the groups to share and then call for a report.

125

7. Point to the third building block: *Your Spirit as a Servant of God*. Ask members to share in pairs the talents and abilities they identified in the activity on pages 100-101 and the spiritual gifts they identified in the activity on page 102. Ask each partner to affirm the other person's abilities and gifts and to add any the person may not be aware of. Ask all members to share how they can dedicate their abilities and gifts to the service of the Lord.

8. Hold up the awl and ask someone to review the information on page 103 about Deuteronomy 15:12-17. Have a dedication service in which each person prays silently: "Father, all I know about me I give to all I know about You. I want to be Your servant for life. I am willing for You to own my life just as a master owns a slave."

9. Distribute a three-by-five-inch card to each member. Ask members to write the names of the persons with whom they shared earlier. Ask them to use the cards as reminders to pray for those persons each day this week. Ask them to pray specifically that the persons will be able to know more about themselves and more about God.

10. Point out the last two building blocks on the session poster: *Things Considered Important in Your Life* and *The People Who Surround Your Life*. Ask how these differ from the first three. (*the first three are internal; these are external.*)

11. Distribute paper and pencils. Ask members to write brief paragraphs based on their study this week that summarize their views toward material things, and describe how they plan to let God use what they have. Let volunteers read their paragraphs.

12. Call attention to the fifth building block. Remind members that just as God owns all material things, He also owns all people. Ask members to suggest guidelines that would help them decide when they are putting their love for another person, including family members, before their love for God.

13. Suggest to members that they need to check where they are on their journey to become ministers. Ask them to share with a partner their answers to the questions on the poster.

14. Close in a prayer of thanksgiving for members' growth during the study. Pray that God will continue to use both victories and setbacks to shape their lives into His image.

------

[1]James E. Taulman, *Help! I Need an Idea* (Nashville: Broadman Press, 1987), 119.

CHRISTIAN GROWTH STUDY PLAN
Preparing Christians to Serve

In the **Christian Growth Study Plan (formerly the Church Study Course),** *Living Your Christian Values* is a resource for course credit in the subject area Personal Life in the Christian Growth category of diploma plans. To receive credit, read the book; complete the learning activities; attend group sessions; show your work to your pastor, a staff member, or a church leader; then complete the following information on the form. This form may be duplicated. Send the completed page to:

Christian Growth Study Plan, MSN 117
127 Ninth Avenue, North
Nashville, TN 37234-0117
Fax: (615) 251-5067

For information about the Christian Growth Study Plan, refer to the current *Christian Growth Study Plan Catalog.* Your church office may have a copy. If not, request a free copy from the Christian Growth Study Plan office, (615) 251-2525.

Living Your Christian Values
CG-0165

PARTICIPANT INFORMATION

Social Security Number (USA ONLY)	Personal CGSP Number*	Date of Birth (MONTH, DAY, YEAR)
– –	–	– –

Name (First, Middle, Last)		Home Phone
☐ Mr. ☐ Miss ☐ Mrs.		–

Address (Street, Route, or P.O. Box)	City, State, or Province	Zip/Postal Code
		–

CHURCH INFORMATION

Church Name

Address (Street, Route, or P.O. Box)	City, State, or Province	Zip/Postal Code

CHANGE REQUEST ONLY

☐ Former Name

☐ Former Address	City, State, or Province	Zip/Postal Code

☐ Former Church	City, State, or Province	Zip/Postal Code

Signature of Pastor, Conference Leader, or Other Church Leader	Date

*New participants are requested but not required to give SS# and date of birth. Existing participants, please give CGSP# when using SS# for the first time. Thereafter, only one ID# is required. **Mail to:** Christian Growth Study Plan, 127 Ninth Ave., North, Nashville, TN 37234-0117. Fax: (615)251-5067

Make the most of every day with the
Everyday Discipleship Series!

The Kingdom Agenda: Experiencing God in Your Workplace

by Mike and Debi Rogers

The world's agenda is to meet needs through self-effort. *The Kingdom Agenda* shows you how to trust God to provide completely for your needs. Wherever you work—at home or in an office, in a factory or on a farm—God loves the people there and wants them in His kingdom. Your workplace is a strategic assignment, a calling to experience God's presence and power all around you. Find out how to develop a prayer strategy for your workplace. Build redemptive relationships and begin cell-group studies using this resource.
0767334086 $7.95

When God Speaks: How to Recognize God's Voice and Respond in Obedience

by Henry Blackaby and Richard Blackaby

This study expands on units five and six of *Experiencing God: Knowing and Doing the Will of God. When God Speaks* teaches adults to discern God's voice, to identify ways He speaks, and to respond to His revelation of His will.
0805498222 $7.95

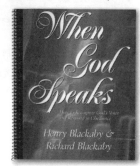

Living God's Word: Practical Lessons for Applying Scripture to Life

by Waylon B. Moore

The most neglected area of Christian living is application of the Bible to daily life. This study helps Christians move from a Bible verse to life change. *Living God's Word* guides readers through prayer, meditation, Scripture memory, claiming God's promises, Bible-study methods, and growing devotional times. Believers will experience a more vibrant faith as they live the truths of God's Word in their daily lives.
0767326040 $7.95

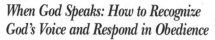

In God's Presence: Your Daily Guide to a Meaningful Prayer Life

by T.W. Hunt and Claude King

Develop a meaningful, balanced, and daily prayer life. *In God's Presence* helps you identify with God in prayer by becoming like Him and by working with Him in prayer. During this study you'll learn about and practice six types of prayer and discover the joy, power, and intimacy that united prayer brings.
0805499008 $7.95